Trend Trading
for a Living

Trend Trading
for a Living

Learn the Skills and Gain the
Confidence to Trade for a Living

Dr. Thomas K. Carr

New York   Chicago   San Francisco   Lisbon   London
Madrid   Mexico City   Milan   New Delhi
San Juan   Seoul   Singapore
Sydney   Toronto

The McGraw·Hill Companies

5 6 7 8 9 0   DOC/DOC   0

ISBN-13: 978–0–07–154419–1
MHID: 0–07–154419–4

This publication is designed to provide accurate and authoritative information in regard to the subject matter covered. It is sold with the understanding that neither the author nor the publisher is engaged in rendering legal, accounting, or other professional service. If legal advice or other expert assistance is required, the services of a competent professional person should be sought.

—From a Declaration of Principles jointly adopted
by a Committee of the American Bar
Association and a Committee of Publishers

McGraw-Hill books are available at special quantity discounts to use as premiums and sales promotions, or for use in corporate training programs. For more information, please write to the Director of Special Sales, Professional Publishing, McGraw-Hill, Two Penn Plaza, New York, NY 10121–2298. Or contact your local bookstore.

All stock charts in this book are used courtesy of Stockcharts.com.

Library of Congress Cataloging-in-Publication Data

Carr, Thomas K.
    Trend trading for a living : learn the skills and gain the confidence to maximize your profits / Thomas K. Carr.
        p.   cm.
    Includes index.
    ISBN-13: 978–0–07–154419–1 (hardcover : alk. paper)
    ISBN-10: 0–07–154419–4
    1. Electronic trading of securities.   2. Speculation.   I.   Title.
HG4515.95.C38   2008
332.64'20285—dc22
                                                                2007030861

This book is dedicated to:

. . . my father, who is a much better pastor than investor, but is supportive of my work nonetheless;

. . . my late mother, who always encouraged her sons to follow their dreams;

. . . my lovely wife, Ina, for looking after our toddler without complaint while I wrote (and for directing me back to the computer when I wasn't writing!);

. . . and my two lovely daughters, Natasha and Nadia, who are my best investments; the risks may be great, but the return on equity is priceless!

CONTENTS

PART FIVE

Trading for a Living

FOREWORD

LET'S talk about your interest in the financial markets. We'll start with the hardest truth of all: it's difficult to turn profits and earn a living through the trading game. After all, no one but the mint is printing money, nor does it grow on trees.

So here's the bottom line for anyone wanting to trade stocks, currencies, or futures. You'll either earn your success through hard work or lose your stake and move on.

Trading has a mathematical advantage over investing, and good traders will make more money over less time than good investors. But the devil is in the details. It's the trader's job to capture volatile price swings that flatten out over the holding period of a buy-and-hold investor. As a result, they need to master the challenging skill of time management.

Take this pursuit seriously, and find a strategy that capitalizes on market movement. Indeed, your success or failure depends on the path you choose. The most dangerous road chases profits without an understanding of downside risk. The safest course builds skills one step at a time and acts defensively when things go wrong.

Fortunately, you've found your way to Thomas Carr's excellent book on trend trading. This informative text opens the market vault to new and experienced traders, welcoming them into our discipline with open arms. Indeed, you'll find everything you need to get started on the road to trading profits in these enlightening pages.

But don't stop your education there. Developing superior trading skills is a lifetime pursuit, in which we're constantly on the hunt for new ideas, methods, and strategies. This active learning process keeps our game fresh in a predatory market world that takes no prisoners.

Make sure your trading matches your lifestyle. You can lose a lot of money when your reach exceeds your grasp. Don't trade every tick if you can't follow the market in real time. Don't day-trade your investments or buy and hold your trades. Never use the market as your therapy for personal problems. It makes a terrible cellmate.

Watch the clock, and become a survivor. Develop a sense of how stocks react to different cycles. Learn the unique traits of the market day, week, and month. These repetitive tendencies affect how prices move and how traders trade. And they reveal telling quirks that produce high-probability trades.

Catalog strange market behavior, and apply simple techniques to trade it. Master a few setups, and let these pay your way while you learn to play the game. Realize that chasing hot stocks is a bad way to make money. Give up the excitement and follow the precision of classic market mechanics. They'll produce consistent profits, with far less stress.

Manage risk before worrying about profits. The most important rule of risk management requires little interpretation: Don't enter a trade without knowing the exit. Understand the risk of your positions, and get out when the price action says you're wrong. Trading small is the best way for new players to control risk until they learn how to make money. Remember that the markets will be there tomorrow, next week, and next year.

Focus on precise entry and exit. Pick your price, and stay on the sidelines when the market doesn't give it to you. Reduce position size when your buying or selling signals don't line up. Use discretion, execute wisely, and remember: good entries on bad stocks produce greater returns over time than bad entries on good stocks.

The best trades come when the information flow sends the same message in different ways. A moving average, news report, and cross-market surge can all suddenly line up and tell you to buy or sell. But avoid seeking out data and opinions just to support your bias. The markets won't care who's on your buddy list when they're ready to move.

Finally, commit many hours of study and observation to the market. Develop a predatory instinct, avoid greed, and view this hobby as a lifelong obsession. Work hard to complete your analysis, and don't cut corners. Develop your own trading style and don't run with the herd.

Be patient, and the doors will eventually open to consistent trading profits.

Alan S. Farley
Author of *The Master Swing Trader*

ACKNOWLEDGMENTS

ACOMPREHENSIVE book like *Trend Trading for a Living* rests on the work of many others, past and present. As a perpetual student of the markets and of trading systems, I am privileged to have had many fine teachers and mentors whose contributions to this volume are evident on every page. Let me take a moment here to acknowledge the most important of those.

I owe a huge debt to the writings of the late Nicholas Darvis, my first and greatest market inspiration, whose story I tell in the Introduction. It was his box system that first got me started in systems development, and it was his breathless story of wealth creation in the stock market while pursuing a full-time career that first inspired me to believe that I could do it, too.

Even more, I am indebted to Alexander Elder, master teacher and market psychologist, also mentioned in detail in these pages. Dr. Elder first revealed to me the elegance and logic of technical analysis as applied to price charts. Many of the key concepts embedded in the systems explained in this text come from his seminal work, *Trading for a Living*, now considered a classic in trading literature.

I also wish to recognize a family friend, the late Gene Browning. Gene was a successful options trader as well as a man of deep faith; he is truly an exemplar of the life well lived. Through several phone conversations, Gene taught me that a career watching numbers and charts need not necessarily exclude a life of devotion to higher principles. Gene was first and foremost a disciple of Jesus Christ. He always saw his trading skills as subservient to that calling.

This book would not exist were it not for Alan Farley, whose commitment to teaching the art of trading to others is second to none. Many years ago Alan embarked on a career as a trader educator through his Web site, Hardrightedge.com, and it was his example and encouragement (at a time when trading was mostly a professional's game with rules unknown to the masses) that inspired me to launch Befriendthetrend.com, now one of the leading online sources of trading education. I am deeply indebted to Alan for volunteering to write the foreword to this book, and I consider it a great honor.

Other important members in the cast of this drama include Jamie Caputo, vice president at RBC/Carlin Equities, whose passion and enthusiasm for supporting traders is as rare as it is contagious; Ken Adams, trading systems developer, superb encourager, and long-term Silicon Investor friend; and Dianne Wheeler, editor extraordinaire, and all her colleagues at McGraw-Hill, for their tireless confidence in this publication and their dedication to publishing professionalism.

A special thanks is owed to all our friends and partners at Befriendthetrend.com: God bless you all!

Trend Trading for a Living

FROM PASSION TO
PROFESSION

BRAINSTORM with me for a minute: what does the stock market represent to you? What images come to mind? What feelings do you associate with trading, with Wall Street, with the global markets? When I reflect on what the markets mean to me, this is what I come up with:

- A free-flowing stream of numbers, numbers, numbers
- Greens and reds, ups and downs, peaks and troughs, ebbs and flows
- A melting pot of products, services, technologies, commodities, and information
- Manhattan high culture, soot-stained buildings, suspenders and pinstripes
- A barometer of the economic and psychological state of the nation, and of the world
- Power, greed, discipline, corruption, intelligence, ecstasy, and agony
- The playground of very energetic people who love making money

- Icon of free-market capitalism, of democracy, of America
- An efficient, highly accessible vehicle for creating wealth, freedom, opportunity

Obviously, my impression of the stock market is an amalgam of a variety of things. The market represents to me the most challenging and most stimulating arena in all of human culture. I love art, literature, architecture, science, film, and fashion. I am a religiously committed person and am conversant with many of the world's major philosophies. But of all products of human making, no other so totally engages my intellect, my will, my *passion* as does the stock market.

My introduction to the stock market came through a recurring image in the pages of my favorite serial comic book character: Richie Rich. There stood the "poor little rich boy" in front of a glass-enclosed machine, slender tape in hand, scrutinizing the ever-growing Rich fortune he was destined to inherit. The neural network this image hardwired into my six-year-old brain must have been permanent, for I have been striving ever since to understand what Master Rich must have understood as he stared at that long stream of paper. If I wanted to live like he lived (and what young boy wouldn't?), I knew I would one day have to unlock the secrets of that mysterious ticker tape.

On my eighth birthday I asked for, and received, the original, 1968 deluxe version of the Whitman Stock Market Game. This classic game is played just like Monopoly, only instead of buying famous streets, you accumulate shares in some of the world's biggest and fastest-growing companies.

At the time, those companies included Maytag, Woolworth, American Motors, International Shoe, and General Mills (how times have changed!). Players barter and bid for shares and are forced to pay dividends when they land on a stock in someone else's portfolio. Unfortunately, I could not get any of my playmates excited enough about the stock market to play with me. So for the most part I played alone, often for hours at a stretch, bidding against myself as I amassed a small fortune. Funny thing, I always won! As an aside, the 1968 Whitman Deluxe Stock Market Game is no longer manufactured, but you can occasionally find one for sale on eBay for about $20.

My next childhood association with the stock market came when I turned 12 and was old enough to walk on my own to the downtown public library after school. The first book I remember checking out with my new library card was a biography of Howard Hughes. I devoured every page, seeing in Hughes a real-life, grown-up version of Richie Rich. While I remember not liking the man very much, I recall wanting to do with my life what he was able to do with his. I remember making the connection in my mind between the ideas of risk, speculation, and passionate investment on the one hand, and on the other, the kind of freedom and power both Rich and Hughes enjoyed.

On my next visit to the library I walked up to the librarian and asked, "Do you have any books on the stock market?" Managing to hide a smile, the woman escorted me quite courteously to a shelf located upstairs in a far, dark corner. After looking over the neatly stacked books, she pulled one down and handed it to me. "Here," she said, "you might like this one." The book's title couldn't have been more perfect: *How I Made $2,000,000 in the Stock Market.* It described how a young professional dancer named Nicolas Darvas amassed a fortune by trading stocks on only three bits of information: the high of the day, the low of the day, and the close. Darvas invested in fundamentally sound, growing companies breaking out of consolidation bases on strong volume. Once he made a purchase, Darvas would simply record the boxes the stock price made as it moved above the base. A box was what Darvas called the trading range the stock tended to trade within, based on its daily highs and lows. If it broke above the upper edge of the box, he would move the box up to a higher level, but if it broke the lower edge of the box, he would sell the stock and cut his losses.

Although I didn't know it at the time, Darvas's book was my first introduction to systems trading—and I was hooked. But I also knew that the kind of fundamental analysis Darvas applied to the companies he traded was beyond the competencies of my 12-year-old brain. So a couple years passed before I picked up another stock market book. When I did, I found a real winner, one that taught me how a profitable system can turn the stock market into a virtual money machine. It was Robert Lichello's 1977 best-seller, *How to Make $1,000,000 in the Stock Market Automatically!* Written in response to the 1970s bear market, Lichello developed a system that exploited the type of volatility that typically appears at market tops and bottoms. Like Darvas's box method, Lichello's system was simple and mechanical: after buying an initial position in a stock, you buy more shares if the price goes down and you sell shares if the price goes up. A mathematical formula was applied to the closing price at the end of each week to determine what to do with your position: buy a little, sell a little, or hold. In this way, Lichello claimed, a stock could move up and down within a range—netting the buy-and-holder very little—and still yield a handsome profit to the one using his automatic investment management (AIM) system.

After I finished Lichello's book I decided to experiment with his system to see whether it worked. I asked my father to explain that odd section of the paper with tiny print that listed all the New York Stock Exchange (NYSE) companies and how they fared in that day's trading. He showed me how to read the numbers and suggested I focus on a company I was familiar with. I chose McDonald's. We ate their hamburgers at least once a week, and though I didn't know that it was the fastest-growing franchise in the United States, I was well aware from the big sign out front that the number of hamburgers served at our local restaurant kept going higher. So I put the AIM method to work with an imaginary 500 shares of McDonald's.

Lichello's AIM method requires only a weekly glance at the closing price of a stock in order to work the system. I decided that was too infrequent, so I checked the price every day. I still remember feeling absolutely elated that first day after my imaginary purchase upon learning that MCD had closed $+\frac{1}{4}$ point, netting me a paper profit of $100. By the end of that first week, as I recall, MCD was up a whole dollar. A $500 return in one week!

The problem with Lichello's method is that it only works with stocks making large up and down swings. However impressive a $1 move might be, it did nothing to trigger AIM's signal to sell shares. That would have required at least a $3 move. So I watched again the next week. Each day I checked the paper to see how my shares did on the big board battlefield, and each day my hopes would rise and fall with each quarter-point advance or decline. This went on for about two more weeks before I finally gave up out of sheer boredom.

I decided to give Darvas's box method another read. I dog-eared the library's copy of *How I Made $2,000,000 in the Stock Market*, carefully taking notes on how to apply every aspect of the system. Again, I took an imaginary investment in my favorite company, McDonald's. It certainly fit the Darvas profile: strong earnings growth, hot prospects, and trading in a long-range base. So early in the summer of 1974 I "bought" 500 shares of MCD in my make-believe trading account and excitedly set about putting Darvas's system to the test. I drew up a kind of primitive spreadsheet for keeping track of the daily highs and lows in order to determine the boxes necessary to manage the open position. At that time, MCD was trading in the low 40s. It had recently broken out of a months-long trading range with a lower edge in the upper 20s and an upper edge in the mid-30s. I already knew MCD was a fundamentally sound company, and this base breakout qualified as a Darvas entry point. So I went long the stock around $42 per share and set my stop-loss just under the lower edge of the new trading range, around $37. About three weeks later, the stock rallied to near $48 before closing the month at $44, so I dutifully moved the Darvas box up two points. My stop-loss now stood at $39, and I was comfortably ahead nearly $1,000. Life was good!

For a while things looked promising. The position came close to getting stopped out following a stern earnings warning, but my box was not touched and I remained in the trade. Then disaster struck. MCD declared earnings that fell below even their lowered prediction, and this was followed promptly by several high-level downgrades. In a swift New York minute I was taken out of the trade for an imaginary, but no less painful, loss of $1,500. Suddenly, and decidedly, my career as a teenage Wall Street tycoon had come to an end.

I grew up a bit after that. I got interested in sports, girls, parties—the usual adolescent distractions. At 18 I went off to university to study medicine, until I discovered I hated being in hospitals and felt nauseated at the sight of blood. So I switched to religious studies and philosophy, and 10 years of graduate study later found myself with a doctorate in the subject, teaching the rudiments of Plato and Aquinas to undergraduates.

Having weathered a very frugal decade as a starving graduate student, and with a mountain of student loans and credit card debt to pay off, not even a full-time professor's salary could tempt me back into the trading game. But when I took up an offer to teach summer school, the $5,000 bonus brought with it, rather unexpectedly, a return of the old trading bug.

The year was 1996 and a new trading tool was all the rage: 24-hour financial television. First came the CNN-Financial Network, and then CNBC and Bloomberg Television. When this input coupled with Internet trading chat rooms, online discount brokers, and cheap charting Web sites, Wall Street quickly became Main Street. The market had just put in a huge year in what was then the middle of the great bull market of the 1990s. Cab drivers shared stock tips, bus boys traded between shifts—the age of the day trader had dawned. The smell of quick profits was in the air, and I wanted to inhale as deeply as possible. So I opened an online brokerage account that summer and put the entire $5,000 into it. In those days, there were no pattern day trader rules, so with $5,000 you could buy up to $10,000 worth of stock on margin and trade it repeatedly throughout the day.

I decided that with such a small amount of capital to work with I had better stick with lower-priced stocks. So I scanned the chat rooms and investor threads for ideas. I soon found one. On all the major sites, traders were buzzing with talk about a small public company that was developing a process by which to turn sewage into safe drinking water. There were rumors that the CEO was going to be interviewed on a network news show sometime that week, and that he would drink a full glass of former sewage in front of the cameras to prove his confidence in his company's system. Speculation ran wild that this exposure to millions of viewers would drive institutional investors to buy up shares in droves.

This seemed about as close to a sure thing as I could find. So I decided to make my first real-money stock purchase in this wastewater treatment company. This small-cap Nasdaq issue was trading around $2.00 at the time, so I bought a starter position of 1,000 shares. I anxiously watched the news that night, but there was no mention of the company. The rumors persisted, and on the next day the stock opened around $2.50. In my euphoria, I bought 1,000 more shares. When just before the close the stock hit a high of $3.00, I bought 1,000 more shares, bringing my position to 3,000 shares at a total investment of $7,500, one-third of which was borrowed from my broker on margin.

That night my heart raced as the news promo mentioned a feature story on a "miracle" water purification system that could revolutionize the way water is used and supplied around the world. This purification process was heralded as having the potential to save the lives of millions of children around the world who would otherwise have no access to clean drinking water. At that moment I clicked onto the discussion thread monitoring the stock and shared in the preannouncement revelry along with dozens of other investors who, like me, had bought thousands of shares in anticipation of this moment. I had never imagined trading stocks could be this easy, or this fun. We were all going to "clean up" on this one, pun intended!

I waited restlessly through the other stories of the evening until Tom Brokaw finally announced the feature we were all waiting for. The preview clip even showed the CEO of an "innovative water treatment company" being challenged by Brokaw to drink a glass of what was formerly sewage, purified by his system. The CEO announced, "Sure, I'll drink that!" With those words, I began a mental process that I have repeated numerous times since: I began calculating what I would do with my sudden windfall. My conservative estimate was that the stock would double overnight, giving me a paper return of at least +125 percent. I planned to sell half my shares and hold the rest as a free trade as the stock ramped up into double digits. With a fresh account of $7,500 in cash, I would then begin stalking my next conquest and do the same thing over again—and again and again—until, like so many of the other day traders I had been hearing about, I would retire young to a seaside mansion and spend my days lounging poolside.

The commercials ended, and Brokaw stood again on screen, ready to introduce the final story of the night. He began by outlining the global problem of polluted water, which accounts for a massive number of deaths in developing nations. With that segue, he ushered in the concept of using ultraviolet radiation along with microfilters to sanitize wastewater. At that moment, there flashed over Brokaw's right shoulder a company logo and name, a company that held the patent on and exclusive marketing rights to a machine that is capable of transforming raw sewage into something that even Evian could bottle. There, plainly visible to millions of television viewers—including hundreds of hedge fund managers, mutual fund analysts, brokers, and day traders—was the logo and name, not of the company whose shares I owned, but of its primary competitor!

Once the initial shock wore off, I immediately plunged into denial. Surely there must have been some mistake. NBC miscued the name of the company, and tomorrow a public relations campaign would swing into action to correct the misinformation. Or perhaps, I quickly reasoned, this is, in fact, very good for our company. People will now invest in the whole sector, and our little company will get swept up in what would become the great water purification bubble of 1996!

As I tuned back in to Brokaw's interview, I watched

intently as the CEO drank a full glass of water taken from his machine. We were told that the water had been reclaimed runoff from the city's drainage system. No doubt this display of confidence in the capacity of the process to produce potable product would go far with industry analysts. I imagined thousands of calls being placed the next day to brokers asking about any and all companies working in this niche market. Again, my euphoria returned.

All was well and good—until Brokaw asked one final question: "So just when will your machine be available to the market?" It was a reasonable question, the kind of question one would expect a top-notch journalist like Brokaw to ask. And to this day every bit of the CEO's answer—the tonality, the meter, the syllabification—remains embedded in my brain. "Oh, the process is too expensive right now to make it marketable." "So . . ." Brokaw pressed, "just how long will it take to get the costs down?" "Well, we are 15, maybe 20 years out," replied the CEO.

And that was it. There was nothing to be done about it. In those days there was no postmarket trading available to make a quick exit. All I could do was wait it out. I knew that throughout the night, traders would start piling up the sell orders, and in the morning at the market's open the price of the stock would plummet—and along with it, all my hopes for early retirement! Sure enough, the stock opened the next day at $1.75 per share, well below my average cost basis for the position. There were far too many orders ahead of mine to get so many shares out easily, and by the time my order filled, I received $1.38 per share, for a loss of over $3,500 if you include the commissions. My trading account was devastated. In a fit of shame and self-disgust, I wired the money out of the account and closed it the next day.

Well, even after that embarrassing experience I simply could not shake the trading bug. The next summer I taught summer school again, and again I opened a small trading account with my extra $5,000. This time, I decided I would do things the right way. I would transform myself into a long-term buy-and-holder, a value investor, a champion of sound fundamentals and fiscal responsibility. I read just enough Lynch, Buffett, Zweig, and O'Neil to know that what I was looking for was a company with that magic combination of regularly increasing earnings, increasing pricing power, lots of cash on hand with little debt, a hot new set of products, and solid growth prospects. I believed the road to market riches lay in finding the next Microsoft, Wal-Mart, or Starbucks before the rest of the investing world. You buy before the growth phase hype hits the streets and then hang on until, after a dozen splits, you sell your nest egg for a small fortune.

Bolstered by this hope, I went searching for the next big thing. What I found was a series of stocks destined, through no fault of their own, to separate me from my hard-earned money. There is no way I could have known it at the time, but that summer of 1997 was not the most opportune time to initiate new long positions. Despite a raging bull market in tech and Internet stocks, the broader markets were overdue for a consolidation, and they sure got one: the S&P chopped sideways for four months and then midyear began a decline that took it 13 percent below its high. It was in that environment that I had determined I would begin my career as a successful long-term investor.

So after several days of research, I bought a small company that provided diagnostic equipment to the airline industry. The stock's press releases referred to the company as holding exclusive contracts with several large carriers. New management on board had been weaned away from successful careers elsewhere. There was little debt and plenty of cash on hand to begin buying up the competition. This company had the smell of Buffettology all over it. It had the right products, under the right management, and with the right business plan to take me and my nest egg to the zenith of financial security; unfortunately, it was in the wrong sector. As profits for the airlines began to dry up, my little company and its exclusive contracts were quickly shown the door. The stock went from $5 per share to under a buck and was then delisted from the Nasdaq, before the company eventually went bankrupt.

Next I bought a boutique electronics dealer with an absurdly low price/earnings (P/E) ratio, no debt, and lots of great press. It had weathered the market pullback well and had recently hired a new CEO. Moreover, the company had just finished a series of small acquisitions, which would ensure their stronghold in the industry. But, as luck would have it, Wal-Mart, Best Buy, and Circuit City were just beginning to expand their operations, and my little firm just couldn't compete. Again, I lost money.

I decided to give the buy-and-hold strategy one more try. With what little cash I had left (about $1,000), I bought into a company that, after DELL and CSCO, was supposed to be the must-own stock of 1997. The stock was in a company that went by the unusually Latinate name of Qualcomm.

In late October, the broader stock indexes had rallied off their lows and looked to be breaking out to new highs. So with what was left of my trading stake, I bet it all on QCOM. Within three weeks, it dropped 40 percent. But this was a long-term hold, so I dutifully held on to my shares. I held the stock for six more months. It went up; it went down. It went up and down again. And again. Finally, at just slightly worse than a break-even price, I sold my shares just to get rid of the nausea. Imagine how heartbroken I felt when less than a year later the stock ramped up by 2,500 percent! Had I held on to those few shares worth around a thousand bucks, I would have had the opportunity to cash out within the year with a quarter-million-dollar nest egg. Arrggh!

It was at this point that I decided to formulate three rules that I have held to ever since:

1. Don't trade on chat room tips.

2. Don't trade on news reports.

3. Don't trade on economic or business forecasts.

I decided that I needed, in all humility, to admit the shortcomings in my preparation as a trader. Although I possess an embarrassing amount of formal education, I am trained in neither economics nor business management. I remember the supply-and-demand curve from my bonehead economics class in college, but the finer intricacies of micro- and macro-economic relationships escape me. Thus, I decided to leave fundamental analysis to the professionals. As for hot stock tips or trading news flashes, there is already a healthy crowd moving in on that action and I've never had much of a liking for crowds.

No, if I was going to succeed in the trading game— and by now this was a matter of resolute determination— I would have to come up with a trading methodology that was well suited to my experiences, my temperament, and the constraints on my time and energy as a full-time professor. Following several weeks of research, I decided that what I needed to learn more about was *technical analysis*, a methodology that relies on simple mathematical relationships along with intuitive price pattern recognition.

Think about this for a moment: fundamental analysis relies on an almost infinite array of inputs, from balance sheets and earnings projections to changes in management, sector cycles, product development, and a whole host of other things too numerous to mention. How can any single human mind, however well trained in business theory, keep track of it all? And not only do you have to know everything about the company you want to invest in, you also have to know everything about its competitors, its sector, its industry . . . and then you have to weigh this knowledge against a background of national, and indeed global, economic analysis. Frankly, who has the time for all that?

Now consider this idea: what if everything you needed to know about a company's future prospects were already there in the price of its shares? This is the key assumption of technical analysis. If the price of your shares is going up, the market likes your company's prospects. If the share price is going down, it doesn't. It's as simple as that. Technical analysis saves a ton of time, is accessible to anyone regardless of education, and, if rightly applied, works pretty darn well.

So I decided then and there that I would focus exclusively on technical analysis to trigger my buy and sell signals. The combination of disciplines inherent to technical analysis seemed to mesh well with my academic training: as a scholar of ancient texts, I had experience both in the objective discernment of linguistic relationships and in the more subjective art of interpretation. Technical analysis seemed to me to be the closest thing to putting these two skills to work on the markets.

Instead of income statements and balance sheets, technical analysts work with price charts. Price charts graphically portray the historical movements of a stock's price and trading volume. They are fixed pictures of a stock's past price behavior over time. The analyst who works with charts is thus part historian, part psychologist, part philosopher: with an experienced eye, she reads the chart to understand its past price patterns, which then allows her to generate a psychological profile of the stock's current state, as well as project a conceptual framework within which the stock is most likely to move going forward. In other words, technical analysts are to the financial world what liberal arts professors are to the world of academia: highly experienced in the arts of evaluation, interpretation, and application.

So with my newfound commitment to learning the finer points of technical analysis, I went in search of mentors. The first thing I did was enroll in a seminar taught by a fellow whose name I won't mention here, since he was later convicted of fraud by the Securities and Exchange Commission (SEC). Nevertheless, while this trader's marketing tactics were suspect, he did, in fact, teach a valid, if basic, technical methodology, the skeleton of which forms the basis of several of the systems outlined in this book. In the seminar I was taught how to use moving averages to determine trend direction and strength, and the stochastics indicator to time entries and exits. To this day, I use both to advantage and consider this particular setup the most reliable of all possible setups. To this fellow I truly owe the foundation of my entire "befriend the trend" system.

An Amazon.com search led me to a second mentor, Alexander Elder. His 1993 best-seller, *Trading for a Living*, now deemed a classic in the field, is a highly readable introduction to both the mathematics and the meaning of the various tools used by technical analysts. Elder is himself a professional psychologist, so I immediately felt at home with someone who, like me, came to the world of trading without a Wall Street or B-school background.

From Elder I learned most of what I now know about the most common technical indicators. I learned what technical oscillators and price patterns tell us about the psychological state of equity markets. I learned about trendlines and how to use them to apply patterns of containment to future movements in price. Most important, perhaps, I learned to recognize and evaluate divergences between price and oscillator behavior. These disjunctions between price trends and the visually portrayed mathematics of those trends provide important psychological clues to the current health and likely forward projection of trends.

Other seminars were to follow. I spent time with Welles Wilder, learning how to combine various indicators with projection trendlines. I learned the finer points of Japanese candlesticks from Steve Nison. In addition to reading all the best-selling books about day trading, I read widely about the stock market itself, the history of Wall Street, and the biographies of several of its biggest players. With these resources under my belt I began to put together and experiment with various technical systems that could be used to recognize profitable market probabilities. It is this set of systems that I am referring to in this book when I talk about *trend trading*. I use the technical systems I have personally developed to determine the nature and strength of a stock's trend, and then use those systems again to alert me to short-term buying and selling opportunities.

There are four different sources of input used in these systems (in no particular order):

- Price patterns (as determined by the use of trendlines and channel lines)
- Moving averages
- Technical oscillators (the exact mix I use changes with the markets, but the core five are MACD, stochastics, RSI, CCI, and OBV)
- Japanese candlesticks

Essentially, successful technical reads of stock charts are all about two things: *present price* and *past price*. Price patterns supply the historical context portrayed by past price that in turn gives meaning to present price. Moving averages give us a visual smoothing of the changing temporal relationship between the two. The various technical oscillators render a visual account of the mathematical relationships between the two. Japanese candlesticks graphically mark the relationship between the current closing price and the range within which the stock traded on an intraday basis.

> **Definition:** A *price trend* refers to the general direction a stock price displays on a price chart when it is moving either up (bullish trend) or down (bearish trend). When a stock is not in a trend but is merely moving up and down within a trading range, we call that a *trendless* or *range-bound* market.

Together, these four vectors map out the relationship between a stock's past and its present state much in the same way the tools of the philosopher (logic, theories of knowledge, metaphysics, etc.) allow him or her to apply ancient wisdom to the issues of the day.

So I set to work hammering out my systems in real-time trading. In order to do this right, I knew I needed the support of an experienced community. To that end, I joined an online trading forum called Silicon Investor. In July of 1998, I started a discussion thread there named "Befriend the Trend Trading," and it soon became one of the most popular threads on the site. In dozens of daily posts, I thought out loud about how to best combine these elements into a series of workable, profitable systems. I posted my picks for the day and followed up with a record of profits and losses. Soon other, more experienced traders joined me, offering their advice and contributing to the overall methodology. We became a tight, mutually supportive network. And within a year, we were consistently, even at times radically, profitable.

Though no one knew it at the time, 1999 will always be remembered—by traders at least—as the year of the infamous tech bubble. The Nasdaq market was ramping up in parabolic fashion. Waiters and barbers were retiring on their investments in Qualcomm, Cisco, Yahoo, and Amazon. Everyone was trading stocks, talking stocks, hyping stocks. Traders were trendy, sexy, and (so everyone thought) rich. They were treated by the media like rock stars, making appearances on *Good Morning America* and *The Tonight Show*. Bankers, doctors, dentists, and lawyers were leaving their six-figure salaries to stay at home, sit in front of computers in their bathrobes, and day-trade. A year and a half later, the markets would crash and *day trading* would become a dirty word. Until that time, however, the party was on and there was no shortage of revelers.

A few made an amazing amount of money in those heady days. One well-known example was Dan Zwanger. In 1999 he turned $11,000 rescued from his greedy but incompetent broker into a $14 million fortune. Another fellow who goes by the name of "Waxie" sold his trading card collection for $150,000, and after his broker reduced it to $30,000, he took control of his portfolio and turned it into $7 million.

We did okay, too. The Silicon Investor thread narrates my experimental venture into the world of high-turnover trading. Because my capacity to stomach market fluctuations is not that strong, I mostly stuck with well-known, larger-cap issues as I continued to refine my systems. We did not yield as much return as the Nasdaq did that year

(+86 percent), but we managed to turn in our first full year of profitable trading.

Then came the year 2000, a year of reckoning. Once all the Y2K fuss had died down, several words that hadn't been heard much the previous year began to be tossed about on the financial shows: words like *valuation*, *sustainability*, and that dreaded "b" word, *bubble*. The intraday volatility increased fivefold as prescient profit takers clashed with bullish latecomers. The get-rich-quick gold rush was over, but it took about six months before most traders and investors realized it. During that time there were regular intraday swings on a scale of wildness that would have made even the late Steve Irwin, the Crocodile Hunter, recoil in fear.

It was in that environment that I began to experiment with a trading system I called BTTT-MAX. BTTT stood for Befriend the Trend Trading (our company name), and the MAX part of the acronym stood for Moving Average Crossover. In this system you were fully invested 100 percent of the time in one or more of the most volatile stocks trading. You watched the intraday hourly chart, and on bullish crossovers, you went long; as soon as a bearish crossover was spotted, you sold the shares and immediately went short. Since in that environment signals came every few hours, and given the violent nature of the intraday swings during that period, BTTT-MAX quickly piled up huge returns.

I'll never forget my first real-money experiment with BTTT-MAX. I was on spring break from the college and spent the week glued to my computer, trading stocks. In my first experiment with MAX, I traded NOVL, then priced in the 30s but headed to single digits before the year was out. I started with 100 shares per side, taking every signal on an hourly basis. After three days of trading I was up nearly $800. Easy money! Encouraged, I added size and began to trade a basket of four stocks per the system. Two days later I was up another $2,200. While my colleagues were out fertilizing their lawns, I had banked a cool three grand simply by clicking my mouse every couple of hours. Nor did the fun stop there. Three months of extreme market volatility managed to exploit the MAX system to such a degree that by the end my account had increased over 500 percent!

Word soon got out about the simple system with the catchy moniker put together by a religious studies professor who was turning a messy market into a pot of gold. The Silicon Investor thread shot to the top of the hot list and stayed there for weeks, and I soon found my phone ringing with requests for interviews. The *Wall Street Journal* wanted to know whether I thought the markets would come back and take out the March 2000 highs. I don't remember now what I said, but I'm sure it was something like this: "It really doesn't matter. What matters is having a great system (like BTT-MAX), which can make money in any kind of market!"

Then *U.S. News and World Report* did a feature story on part-time day traders, using me as their poster child. The story included a full-page color spread of "Dr Stoxx" sitting in his cramped college office. Unbeknownst to me, the story intended to focus on losing traders, and since I was coming off a hard week my only quote after a three-hour interview was about losing $1,500 on a JNPR trade.

After that, I wised up to the fact that the media wished to portray traders negatively (as greedy, irresponsible, sociopathic dropouts), and so I declined all further interviews.

As seasoned traders know well, a system like BTTT-MAX, which exploits particular market conditions, works well only until those conditions change. Sure enough, they did, and our profits began to dry up. I have since refined the system to keep us out of the markets when conditions are not right, but I doubt we will ever see returns with the system like we saw in that magical summer of 2000.

In the years since the market's bubble burst, since those ecstatic days of BTTT-MAX, I've been hard at work expanding the universe of Befriend the Trend Trading systems. In 2002 we launched our Web site, Befriend-thetrend.com, along with a free weekly newsletter designed to highlight one new stock pick each week derived from whatever system was working best at the time. Today, five years on, we are still going strong, with over 7,000 subscribers to that original newsletter. Over the years we have launched three additional newsletters for paying subscribers and have seen brisk sales on the six trading manuals we have published and two seminars we've held. Our latest venture began in March of 2005, when I incorporated a capital management company and partnered with RBC Carlin Equities and Goldman Sachs to oversee the Befriend the Trend Fund for accredited investors. Yes, I still teach (and enjoy teaching) undergraduate students at the college the finer points of philosophy and religion.

Nothing has been easy since the nearly vertical market ramp-up of the late 1990s. The broader indexes have been trading within tighter and tighter ranges, as the SEC and

Federal Reserve are quicker to clamp down on excesses. Currently, as I write this, various markers for market volatility (the VIX, Bollinger Band Width, option premiums, etc.) are just beginning to rise off historic lows. Global and local economies have had to discount things like terrorism, rising oil prices, and natural disasters. The current buzzword among market prognosticators is not *valuation* or *bubble* but *geopolitics*. Day traders are out, and hedge fund managers— a far more powerful influence on market volatility—are in. Recently, both Merrill Lynch and Goldman Sachs fired dozens of traders because they were not making any money. The markets are just that tough!

The good news is that in any market condition, with the right systems at hand, trading can nicely supplement your income, and if you have the patience to stick with it for a while, it can even make you very wealthy. It takes some work getting up to speed on the terminology. Learning to read a chart is a little bit like learning a foreign language. But the hard part has been done for you. You hold in your hands the culmination of years of intensive labor, done on your behalf. Here you have all the information you need to find stocks poised to move, to take positions in those stocks, and to exit those positions with the greatest exposure to profit and the least exposure to risk. The trading systems outlined here have been designed to be as close to 100 percent mechanical as possible. And each system is complete. You are not taught here a few fundamental principles and then left on your own to apply them to the markets. I've done all the necessary applicational steps for you. All you have to do is copy my work.

All of this is to say: if I can do it, so can you! Regardless of your education, your trading experience, your flu-
ency with numbers, you, too, can trade for a living. Can
you tell whether a line is moving up or down? Can you
click a mouse? Then you, too, can trade for a living. We at
Befriendthetrend.com wish you all the best as you start this
wonderful adventure of trend trading.

PRELIMINARIES

PART ONE

CHAPTER 1

WHAT YOU NEED TO
GET STARTED

T REND trading is the ideal home-based business. There is no inventory to store in warehouses, nothing to ship, no bothersome customers, no cold calling, no gimmicky marketing. You don't have to haunt garage sales and flea markets looking for items to sell on eBay. Unlike real estate investing, traders don't have to worry about doing any maintenance work or tracking down renters who are late with their payments. There is no Wal-Mart down the road to undercut your prices. There are no franchise fees, no staff to employ, no lawyers to keep on retainer.

Yes, there is a certain amount of starting capital required, and yes, there are some monthly costs that will make a small dent in your profits. Compared to most other home businesses, however, trend trading has as low a set of barriers to entry as any business could possibly have. Profit margins run well over 90 percent. It's hard to beat that!

All you really need to trade profitably and comfortably are a good chair, a newer computer with a wide-screen monitor, a high-speed Internet connection, some software, a calculator, and paper and pen. That's it. I'm guessing that many of you reading this will already have most if not all of these items, but if you do not yet have them, let me offer some guidance on the more important ones.

HARDWARE

I recommend using a recent-model desktop PC or Macintosh computer. Between these two formats, the Windows-based option is the better choice, since most of the software useful for trading is available only in that format. With the recent success of newer and faster Mac computers, this may change in coming years, but for now the widest selection of trading software can be found only for the Windows platform.

Regarding the computer, processor speed is not as important as memory capacity. To be sure, the faster the processor speed, the better. The fact is, though, that even the cheapest new PC today is plenty fast enough to handle what you will need for trading. Memory, however, should not be skimped on. With a large amount of random-access memory (RAM), you will be able to run your trading platform, charting software, news feed, and a couple of Web browsers all at once without running the risk of freezing your machine due to overload. RAM capacity of 500MB is sufficient to run most trading platforms and charting packages simultaneously, but a doubling of that would nearly guarantee a flawless trading experience.

The monitor is also an important piece of your trading arsenal. As a rule, the larger the monitor, the better. For this reason, laptops are not the best choice for trading. They are fine for those days you are on the road and need to keep tabs on your portfolio. I find myself frequently trading from the local Starbucks on a laptop with wireless broadband connection. But try opening your trading workstation, your real-time charts, a quote streamer, your watch lists, and your Befriend the Trend newsletters all at once, and you will soon realize how necessary it is to have as much desktop space as possible. Some traders use more than one monitor to trade from, and if you can afford it this is not a bad idea. You may need to install a dual video card to handle more than one screen, but the small investment will be worth it.

There are also multiscreen and tiling screen monitors now that are designed especially for traders. These can give you up to 100 diagonal inches of desktop space: a genuine luxury. They are expensive, however, running over $5,000 each for the better models. As for me, I use a single, 24-inch flat-panel, high-definition monitor and do not consider this at all hazardous to my trading. But try to trade every day on a tiny 14-inch screen? No way!

If you are interested in multiple monitors and can afford it, take a look at a company called Digital Tigers (assuming they are still in business). They produce multipanel monitors with as many as seven separate panels, including a television display. Imagine having CNBC on one panel and Bloomberg on another panel, with additional panels devoted to your trading platform, a variety of your favorite charts, and browsers open to trading chat rooms, discussion threads, and your Befriend the Trend Newsletters. Now that is trading heaven! They also manufacture a product called a *sidebar*, which allows you to plug a multiple monitor into your laptop (though then it is no longer a laptop, is it?).

SOFTWARE

Where you go with software will depend greatly on what kind of capital you are starting with in your trading account. If you are trading under $10,000, then you will need to find ways to get your streaming data and charts for as little cost as possible (remember, I started out with only $5,000). If, however, you can fund your account with up to $25,000, then you can afford to step up to the next level, and I'll show you how. If you are fortunate enough to plunk over $50,000 of risk capital into your account, then let me show you the sort of premium services that will serve your trading well.

The truth is, you really do not need to spend any money at all on software to have all the tools you need to trade safely and profitably. There are free services galore in the trading world. And among the fee-based providers, many will let you download their basic services without paying. Of course, they hope you will like their entry format so much that you will be willing to pay for the upgrade. But in most cases you will have all the information you need to trade the markets profitably without much in the way of overhead costs.

Among the free services, your first stop should be Stockcharts.com. Stockcharts.com offers a fantastic Web-based technical charting service that you can use for free. Simply by signing up you will have access to 20-minute delayed charts with a wide variety of technical indicators, limited stock scans you can use to find setups, sector and market breadth analysis, and much more. Their candle-glance feature allows you to create and save an infinite number of small charts that you can use as your primary watch lists (explained later). With low-cost upgrades, Stockcharts.com will allow you to access real-time charts and scan for an unlimited number of setups.

Real-time quotes should be available from your broker, but if, like me, you like a freestanding quote streamer, you should download a copy of Jerry Medved's award-winning Quotetracker software. It is free and compatible with dozens of data sources, including most online brokerages and real-time charting packages. Quotetracker includes Level II quotes, real-time intraday charts, price alerts, and a news feed—all for free! The software is ad-supported, so you will have to put up with periodic banners and pop-up ads, but for a very small monthly fee (about the price of one trade commission) you can use a version without the ads. For further information and to download the software, just go to Quotetracker.com.

If you wish to take your trading to the next level and want that extra measure of control over your entries and exits, then you will need a real-time charting package. While Quotetracker offers real-time charts for free, many do not find the charting format very user friendly. The same can be said for the charts offered by most online brokers. Instead, I would recommend moving up to IQCharts. As a midpriced service, IQCharts offers a real-time, stand-alone charting package that includes all the indicators you will need, intraday charts that automatically update in real time, the ability to store dozens of watch lists with slide-show capabilities, and both pre-packaged and construct-your-own scans with technical and fundamental parameters. IQCharts is also one of the only real-time charting packages currently available for the Macintosh platform.

Another midpriced option is TC2000. In addition to a real-time charting system, TC2000 offers stock advisory guidance from the company's founders, the Worden brothers. They also have a community feature where stock traders can chat with each other in real time about what they are trading, and the Worden brothers themselves offer free daily market commentary to all paying subscribers.

The highest level of trading sophistication comes with a price tag. If you can afford about $125 per month for your real-time charts (more if you want futures data), then there are three packages I can recommend: Quote.com, eSignal, and RealTick. I've used all three services, and while there are a few minor differences between them, I don't have a clear favorite. These services will take some time to get used to if you have been trading on a more scaled-down format. Once you get used to it, though, you'll wonder how you ever traded on anything less. If you plan on day trading any of our trend-trading systems, then I strongly recommend going with either of these two premium services.

There are many other forms of trading software you can purchase, but I'm convinced that other than your broker's trading platform, a basic membership with Stockcharts .com, and a real-time charting package, *there is nothing else you need for trading profitably*. However, there are traders for whom research is half the fun of trading. For them there is no shortage of software and Web-based services one can purchase or subscribe to that will seemingly enhance their ability to investigate every possible technical, economic, cyclical, and fundamental angle of the markets.

Two such services I can recommend are MetaStock, which is a high-end package that, among other things, will allow you to backtest your technical trading systems, and VectorVest, which analyzes and ranks the universe of stocks every day according to certain fundamental and technical parameters. Again, however, to trade well all you really need to spend is between $10 and $50 per month for the few basic services listed here.

INTERNET SERVICE PROVIDERS

When it comes to Internet service providers these days, you have a lot of choices. There is dial-up, high-speed dial-up, HSDN, DSL, satellite broadband, cable broadband, and T-1 lines. I've always used a cable ISP and would not want to trade on anything slower. But then, I do a fair amount of day trading where speed and a constant flow of data are essential.

Many subscribers to our BTTT Newsletters trade with dial-up and do just fine. To enter your trade orders and monitor your open positions, dial-up is normally sufficient. Fortunately, trading hours for most U.S. time zones at least do not coincide with those dreaded "porn hours" (late evening) when the phone lines get jammed and data runs slowly. If you are a subscriber to one of our newsletters (or any newsletter service, for that matter), you won't need the surfing speed required to do all the stock research. However, if you plan on doing your own research—running your market scans and checking your watch lists each day—you will save yourself countless hours of surf time by switching to a broadband provider of some kind.

I am on the road a lot during the year and nearly always stay in hotels that have high-speed Internet access, but occasionally I have to resort to using dial-up. It works just fine as long as you don't need to be lightning fast when entering and exiting trades. I also recommend keeping a dial-up service installed and paid for as a backup during those inevitable times when your cable or other higher-speed service goes on the blink. To this end, I can recommend using NetZero's high-speed dial-up service. For $15 per month you have the security of knowing that you are only a phone line away from being able to put on and take off trades.

One final option to look into is a satellite service that runs through your wireless phone connected by modem to your laptop. This can be a bit expensive, with monthly costs running up to near $100, and in the recent past they were too slow to be cost effective. However, the current versions are much faster, and with this setup you can take your laptop nearly anywhere in the world and set up your trading workstation.

ONLINE BROKERS

Just a few quick words about your online broker: you need a good one, an inexpensive one, and one whose system for inputting trades you are comfortable with. In my years of trading, I've used most of the popular online brokerages: Schwab, Datek, E*Trade, Suretrade, Scottrade, Investrade, Interactive Brokers, and MB Trading (some of these are no longer in operation). All offer discount pricing—though some are more discounted than others—and user-friendly trading and account management interfaces.

Currently I have a personal account with Interactive Brokers (IB) and trade the Befriend the Trend Fund through a prime broker (Goldman Sachs, which uses the REDIPlus platform). I recommend IB to anyone. I have found them to be reliable and inexpensive ($1 or less per 100 shares traded), and their account management system is user friendly. Some people, however, find their Trader Workstation, which is where you input your trades, cumbersome and confusing.

A recommended alternative is MB Trading. They offer the same price structure as Interactive Brokers, but they also offer a $9.95-per-trade option for unlimited shares. This is an attractive option for larger accounts or those trading penny stocks. Generally I find their MBT Navigator, where trades are inputted, to be slightly more user friendly than IB's Trader Workstation, though IB's recent upgrades to their system make the differences between the two formats minimal.

CHAPTER 2

BECOMING A
CHART READER

IN the chapters that follow, I am going to reveal exactly what I look for when I select new trades to be included in the various Befriend the Trend Trading newsletters. An important point to remember: selecting stocks to trade is the easy part. Knowing when to enter and exit is the hardest part, and the most important part, of trading. Both how to enter and how to exit your positions will be discussed in detail here.

Before we get to the nuts and bolts of how you can actually begin to put your money to work in the markets, however, we first need to discuss the most important element of all trading that is based on technical analysis: the price chart. In this section I will tell you exactly how I set up and read the charts I use for selecting new trades and monitoring open positions.

THE INDICATORS

The first thing you should do is set up your default chart with all the indicators and parameters you will need to make technically sound trading selections. For myself, I use two sets of charts: I make frequent reference to a delayed charting service offered by Stockcharts.com and consider their charts to be the best Web-based service available. With their basic subscription (about $10 per month), you can set up your charts with all the parameters and indicators I teach here as well as screen for the setups taught later in the book. Their charts are also easy to read and can be formatted to suit a variety of aesthetic tastes. Recently, Stockcharts.com added real-time data to their subscription service for a small additional monthly charge. While the charts do not update instantly as they do in the premium services listed previously, you can set the charts to update automatically every 15 seconds.

The second package I use is eSignal's premium charting service with real-time stocks, options, and futures data. With eSignal you can input an infinite number of watch lists, and with a simple click of the mouse you can scroll through these easily in real time. While the package I subscribe to is fairly expensive and constitutes a considerable overhead cost, the advantages it affords are worth it. With the eSignal premium package, you can get automatically updating charts with real time in all time frames, and with what I consider to be the most readable format available.

If you use eSignal or a similar service, like Quote.com or RealTick, for your charting needs, you have the opportunity to set up several charts that will simultaneously display different time periods for the same stock symbol. At the click of the mouse, you can change from stock to stock as you view weekly, daily, and various intraday charts for each stock side by side. Less sophisticated charting packages such as IQCharts and TC2000 also allow for multiple charts in different time frames, but the linkages between them are not as intuitive and are often buggy and unstable. For most trading purposes this is sufficient, but where you need the edge of split-second decision making, there is no substitute for higher quality.

Whatever charting service you use, you should add the following indicators to your default chart:

- Simple moving averages (SMAs): 20 MA, 50 MA, 200 MA
- Moving average convergence-divergence (MACD): 12–26–9 periodicity
- Stochastics: 5–3 (or 5–3–3) periodicity
- On balance volume (OBV)
- Relative strength index (RSI): 5 periodicity
- Commodity channel index (CCI): 20 periodicity

If you are confused at this point, don't worry. Here is a simple primer on what these indicators mean and how they tend to be used.

Simple Moving Averages (SMAs): 20, 50, and 200 Settings

- *Theory:* An MA measures the consensus, or average, closing price of a stock over a given period of time. A 20 setting shows the average price over 20 days, and so on. A simple MA is one that takes an equally weighted average of price.
- *Reading the indicator:* SMAs represent price consensus over a given period of time. When

price gets too far away from the consensus, it
tends to revert to that consensus like a magnet. In
turn, SMAs tend to act as barriers to price,
putting a stop to any trend that runs into it.
SMAs also indicate trend: if they are sloped up,
the price trend is up (bullish). If they are sloped
down, the price trend is down (bearish). If the
slope is sharp, the trend is strong, and if the slope
is shallow, the trend is weak. A flat or choppy
SMA indicates a range-bound market.

- *Uses:*
  1. To show areas of support and resistance
  2. To determine the direction and strength of the
     current trend

- *Chart example:* Figure 2.1 shows the S&P 500
  proxy (SPY) with both the 20 (dotted line) and
  the 50 (solid line) SMAs overlaid. Note how the

Figure 2.1   Dow Jones Industrial Average with 20/50 SMAs.

upward slope on the left of the chart confirms the
uptrend in price and acts as support for that
uptrend, while the right of the chart shows the
SMAs confirming a breakdown in price. The flat
50 SMA in the right third of the chart indicates a
choppy, range-bound market.

Moving Average Convergence/Divergence (MACD): 12–26–9 Periodicity with Histogram (a Bar Graph of Daily MACD Readings) Overlay

- *Theory:* MACD measures the difference between a
  shorter-term consensus of price and a longer-term
  consensus, and works on the assumption that when
  these diverge, the current price trend is increasing
  in strength, and when they converge, the trend is
  decreasing in strength. The periodicity settings
  represent the following: a 12-day moving average
  of price (short-term), a 26-day moving average
  (longer-term), and a 9-day average of the
  difference between the two averages.
- *Reading the indicator:* Positive MACD readings
  (above the 0-line) indicate that bulls are in charge
  of the market, while readings below the 0-line
  indicate that bears are in charge. The length of
  the histogram bars can be used to determine the
  strength of trends: the longer the bars, the
  stronger the trend (and vice versa). Also, both the
  MACD signal lines and the MACD histogram
  can be used to show bullish or bearish divergence

from price, which can give tradable signals (the term *divergence* will be explained later). Crossovers from positive to negative MACD readings, and vice versa, do not offer reliable trading signals, since they tend to lag the market.

- *Uses:*
    1. As a contrarian indicator when it diverges from price
    2. To determine the strength or weakness of price trends
    3. To determine whether a market is currently bullish or bearish
- *Chart example:* In Figure 2.2, the SPY has the MACD below it, showing an interesting relationship between indicator and price. Note how as

Figure 2.2   SPY with MACD indicator.

the uptrend matures, MACD fails to put in new highs even as price does so. This indicates relative weakness, or *bearish divergence*. Also note the moves above and below the 0-line with respect to price moves. Clearly these shifts cannot be used as trading signals since they come too late to catch the move, but they are valuable in indicating the overall mood (bullish or bearish) of the stock's price.

Stochastics: 5 (%K), 3 (%D) Settings

- *Theory:* Stochastics measures the relationship between the most recent closing price and the total price range (highs to lows) over a given period of time. A declining stochastics indicates that price is tending to close near the lower end of its recent trading range (bearish), while a rising stochastics indicates that price is tending to close near the upper end of its recent trading range (bullish). %D is a moving average of %K values over a given period.
- *Reading the indicator:* Stochastics gives a clear buy signal once it passes below the 20-line (oversold) and then %K crosses over %D. It gives a clear sell signal once it passes above the 80-line (overbought) and then %K crosses under %D.
- *Uses:*
    1. To register overbought and oversold levels in price
    2. To register entry and exit signals for trend trades

Figure 2.3   SPY with stochastics indicator.

3. As a contrarian indicator when it diverges from price

- *Chart example:* In Figure 2.3, the SPY has the stochastics (5–3) below it. Note how dips to or below the 20-line (oversold) often precede sharp upward thrusts in price. The signals to sell over the 80-line (overbought) are less reliable during the uptrend, but offer profitable trading opportunities once the index shows some weakness in the overall trend.

On Balance Volume (OBV)

- *Theory:* Since OBV is measured by adding the volume of an up day to a running total of volume and subtracting the volume of a down day from that total, it gives us a pictorial image of whether a stock is being accumulated (more shares being bought than sold) or distributed (more shares sold than bought) over time. A rising OBV indicates accumulation, while a falling OBV indicates distribution.

- *Reading the indicator:* If a price trend is confirmed by supportive volume, OBV will move in concert with price, making new highs or lows along with new price highs or lows. When it does so, OBV confirms the current trend. When it does not, OBV acts as a contrarian indicator. OBV sometimes acts as a leading indicator: if it rises ahead of price, price tends to follow; and vice versa if it falls ahead of price.
- *Uses:*
  1. To confirm the validity of current trends and breakout moves
  2. As a contrarian indictor signaling false breakouts and weakening trends
  3. As a leading indicator useful to taking positions in breakouts prior to the breakout move
- *Chart example:* In Figure 2.4, the SPY has OBV below it. OBV is used to confirm price trends, so as long as OBV is making new highs, the bullish price trend should be bought. But note how OBV gave a divergence warning in late February when it failed to print a new high as price was hitting new highs. The market sold off sharply right after that. The OBV was right—traders were distributing their shares.

Figure 2.4   SPY with the OBV indicator.

Relative Strength Index (RSI): 5-Period Setting

- *Theory:* RSI is measured by dividing an average of net positive changes in closing prices over a given period of time by an average of net negative changes in price. As this number increases over time, a bullish trend is confirmed. When the number decreases, a bearish trend is confirmed.

- *Reading the indicator:* RSI should move in concert with price during major trends. When RSI diverges from price, this represents a tradable situation and may indicate a top or bottom to the current trend. A reading above 70 indicates overbought levels in price, while a reading below 30 indicates oversold levels in price.

- *Uses:*
  1. As a contrarian indicator, foreshadowing potential reversals of trend
  2. To confirm the validity of the current trend or price breakout
  3. To register overbought and oversold levels in price
- *Chart example:* In Figure 2.5, the SPY has RSI below it. Like other oversold-overbought indicators, RSI can be used profitably to alert us to buy and sell signals, but only when other

Figure 2.5 SPY with the RSI indicator.

factors are in place. As a stand-alone indicator, it is best used to show divergence. On the chart in Figure 2.5, we can see clear bearish divergence to price in late February and bullish divergence in the middle of March.

Commodity Channel Index (CCI): 20-Period Setting

- *Theory:* CCI is calculated by dividing price increases or decreases over a period of time by a mean standard deviation of a consensus or average of price over time. The resulting plotted line of this calculation will give visual readings of the strength of current trends as well as indicate "hidden" strength or weakness during relatively flat market periods.
- *Reading the indicator:* Extreme high and low readings in the CCI indicator (+200/–200) are used by some traders to signal price waves or cycles. The indicator can also be used, like other single line indicators (RSI, OBV), to signal buys and sells when the indicator diverges from price. Like other indicators, CCI can be a leading indicator when it diverges from price. A relatively flat market with a rising or falling CCI can signal future direction in price.
- *Uses:*
  1. As a contrarian indicator, foreshadowing potential reversals of trend
  2. To confirm the validity of the current trend

3. To indicate the beginning and end of price
   waves or cycles within a larger trend

- *Chart example:* In Figure 2.6, SPY has the CCI
  indicator below it. Again like the RSI indicator,
  we see bearish divergence in late February
  and bullish divergence in mid-March. What
  is unique about CCI is its ability to pinpoint
  cycle changes. The extreme bearish reading we
  see at the end of February and beginning of
  March signals a change of cycle. The short-
  lived bearish cycle is likely over, and a new
  bullish cycle has begun.

Figure 2.6   SPY with the CCI indicator.

So that's it. These "sexy six" are the only indicators I use consistently in all my trend-trading systems. There are other indicators I occasionally use, such as a five-period exponential MA coupled with an eight-period SMA, Bollinger Bands, ADX, and Money Flow, but these are used mostly in special-case trading situations that fall outside the parameters of ordinary, everyday trend-trading strategies. For most trend-trading purposes, the preceding list is sufficient.

SETTING UP YOUR CHART

Now it is time to set up your chart. The foregoing gives you a list of all the indicators you should put on your primary chart, along with the specific settings. These indicators and settings will remain the same whether you are looking at weekly, daily, or intraday charts. The trend-trading systems you will learn in this book can be applied to all time frames, depending on your trading preferences and goals. But for the purposes of simplicity, we will limit our examples to the daily chart.

Some of these indicator settings are configured to the standard default setting you get with most charting applications. But several (stochastics, RSI, CCI) have been set to a more sensitive reading, which better supports what we are trying to do with trend trading. You can fiddle around with these numbers if you want to, but I recommend at least trying the settings I use first.

Figure 2.7 is a chart of the S&P 500 proxy SPY (Spyders) with all the aforementioned indicators. Take note of several things.

Figure 2.7 SPY with all the indicators.

1. First, look at how the MAs (20, 50, and 200) went from a period of up and down confusion, crossing over each other and not giving much of an indication of trend, to a period where all three are sharply rising, with the 20 (dotted line) over the 50 (thick solid line) and the 50 over the 200 (thin solid line). This change of condition we call a change from a *range-bound* to a *strongly uptrending* market. Both these terms will be defined in greater detail in the next section.

2. Note the oversold and overbought conditions of the RSI, stochastics, and CCI indicators and compare these values to what price did. Not every oversold or overbought condition marks a valid buy or sell signal. Indicators need to be taken together with other triggers on the price chart itself. Oversold and overbought conditions can simply become very oversold or very overbought before they resolve themselves. As a clear example of this, compare the consistently overbought action of stochastics during the month of November with what price was doing (i.e., going up and up).

3. Note how the OBV indicator can be played with trendlines—just like price. A breakout of the downtrend line in early November signaled the start of a healthy bull run, while the break of the uptrend line in mid-January may signal a new downtrend in price.

4. Note how CCI marked significant cycle changes whenever it hit extremes of +/−200. Except for the November high, the other three signals circled on the chart proved profitable. CCI can also be played like OBV, with trendlines overlaid. The trendline break to the upside in mid-October signaled a buying opportunity.

5. Finally, note the bearish divergence that crept into the last two months of trading. Note how even though the SPY price was making new near-term highs, the RSI and MACD indicators were making lower highs. This is bearish divergence and flashes a caution sign to market bulls. Indeed, several weeks later SPY traded down to near 120.00 before recovering.

Figure 2.8 is another chart of the S&P 500 proxy, SPY, from a year earlier than the chart that preceded it. Here I have highlighted a number of divergences between price and the various indicators we use. Whenever price sets a higher high or lower low without the indicators following suit, we have a setup that often foreshadows large market moves. When divergence is seen between price and one or more indicators, trend traders will fade the price and trade in the direction of the indicators. Also note again the use of trendlines on the OBV indicator and how a break of those lines can signal a change in price direction. And finally, take a look at how the indicators, especially stochastics, register oversold and overbought conditions at or near major market reversals.

Figure 2.8 SPY with all the indicators.

TRENDLINES AND CHANNEL LINES

It is extremely important in trend trading to determine whether the market in general, and the stocks on our watch lists in particular, are in a trend, and if so, what kind of trend it is. Trendlines and channel lines are among the tools we use to do this.

Trendlines and channel lines are lines drawn over at least two tops and under at least two bottoms of major price movements. The more tops and bottoms you can intersect with the trendline, the more valid the trend. As a general rule, we recommend only drawing in a trendline that can intersect at least three price points. Note that these price points need not be pivots in price (that is, highs and lows in price), merely touches of the trendline by individual price bars.

Trendlines help traders identify the dominant trends that price has tended to trade within, while channel lines demarcate trendless channels or trading ranges with support and resistance points. In short, these lines give us a simple, visual reference as to whether the stock is in an uptrend or a downtrend, or is stuck in a trading range. Furthermore, if we extend those lines beyond the right edge of the chart, we will have a visual map of where the stock is likely to trade into the near future. Thus, trendlines are an invaluable tool in helping us to make profitable trading decisions.

Trendlines are used to measure uptrends by drawing the lines under the lows, while downtrends are measured by drawing the lines over the highs. A series of higher lows indicates that the bears are getting less aggressive and the bulls more confident. That is all we need to know to call such movement an uptrend. The reverse is true for a downtrend. An uptrending line drawn below the lows combined with a flat line over the highs is still an uptrend. A downtrending line over the highs combined with a flat line under the lows is still a downtrend. Again: In an uptrend, only the lows count. In a downtrend, only the highs count.

The following are theoretical examples of both an uptrend and a downtrend. Note that the trend is determined by only one side of the formation: the lows for the uptrend and the highs for the downtrend. Figure 2.9 is an example of an uptrend. Figure 2.10 is an example of a downtrend.

If both trendlines—the one over the highs and the one under the lows—are flat, the stock is in what we call a trading *channel* or trading *range*. The stock's price is likely to bounce up and down between these channel lines until either the upper or the lower line is broken. If the upper

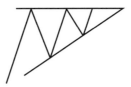

Figure 2.9   An uptrend defined by higher lows, not higher highs.

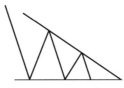

Figure 2.10   A downtrend, defined by lower highs, not lower lows.

line is broken, we can expect to see a new uptrend develop. If the lower channel line is broken, we can expect to see a new downtrend develop. The same principles apply when we have an uptrending line under the lows combined with a downtrending line over the highs. This is still a channel, but it is now what we call a *narrowing channel* or a *triangle* formation. Any breakout from that formation is a tradable event.

Figures 2.11 and 2.12 are theoretical examples of the two most common types of trading ranges or channels.

Both trendlines and channel lines are used in following ways:

- To determine the status of a price trend: up, down, or range-bound
- To project future points of price resistance and support
- To calculate where to put stop-losses
- To note areas of price containment in order to predict breakout moves

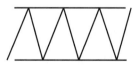

Figure 2.11   A sideways trading channel or range.

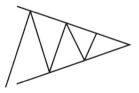

Figure 2.12   A tightening trading range or triangle.

Figure 2.13   BRCM showing trendlines.

Figure 2.13, the BRCM chart, demonstrates a trading channel or range in August that broke out to the upside.
This led to choppy trade with short-term up- and downtrends, which then led to a more prolonged downtrend in
October, followed by a prolonged uptrend into December.
Note that if a position had been taken during either the
channel or any of the trending patterns, the stop-loss for
shorts should have been placed just over the upper trendline (dotted line) and a stop-loss for longs just under the
lower trendline (solid line) once the trendline was established with at least three points of intersection.

Figure 2.14 is a classic trading range or channel
breakout exhibited by BEAS. The stock bounced up and
down within a 2.00 range for five months before finally
breaking out to the upside. This kind of long-term price
containment with breakout sends the bullish signal that
the stock is now ready to trade within a higher price range.

Figure 2.14   BEAS showing price channel breakout.

Note also that once the price channel was established by sufficient price touches in late July, the lower trendline, once extended out to the right, would have been a reasonable place of support to put a bid in for the stock (and the same would be true for putting an offer at the upper trendline). Note finally that the break of the second established trading range's lower trendline in early November signaled that it was time to exit the trade and bank the profit. This chart thus represents a potential trend trade return of over +40 percent in about nine weeks: buying BEAS at trendline support (near 11.00) and selling on a trendline break near 15.50.

Two warnings need to be issued regarding the use of trend and channel lines. The first is that these lines are always subjectively drawn. Even when software is used to draw trendlines, there is subjectivity at work in the way the programmer coded the software. This is to say that you must always be ready to alter your trend-lines in response to new market data. It is all too easy to draw in a trend channel where none really exists because we have a predisposed bias to the stock moving in a certain direction. Trendlines and wishful thinking are a dangerous combination. For this reason, always apply the following rule to your use of trend and channel lines:

> No trend or trading channel exists until a line can be placed on the chart that intersects at least three price points. Two price points can yield a trendline, but no trading decision should be made until a third touch of the line is recorded.

There is much debate among market technicians and traders whether one should run a trend or channel line over/under intraday prices (the "tails" or "shadows" on the candlesticks) or only the end-of-day price points. There are various answers to this question. It has been my general experience that closing prices trump intraday swings. Thus, if you draw a trend or channel line across the tops or under the bottoms of several runs in price, and then find that at numerous points there are intraday swings in price that cannot be contained by those lines, it is okay. As long as you contain within the lines the majority consensus represented by the closing price (or the edge of the candle body if you are using candlestick charts), I believe you can more or less ignore the extreme opinions represented by a few wayward intraday runs (or tails). Some do prefer, however, to use lines to contain all points in price, including intra-

Figure 2.15   RIMM with trendlines.

day swings. Hence, a sound compromise position on drawing trendlines can be heard in the teaching of Alexander
Elder, who states, ". . . It is better to draw [the line]
through the edges of congestion areas. Those edges show
where the majority of traders have reversed direction."
(Elder, p. 88)

   In Figure 2.15, the chart of RIMM demonstrates
Elder's trendline technique in action. Here we see a downtrend line and subsequent uptrend line passing through
areas of price congestion rather than at either intraday or
end-of-day price points.

   A second warning with respect to trend and channel
lines is that traders often have the tendency to draw too
many of them. If we keep in mind that such lines are
merely accidental tools we use to give us a very general
sense of price containment and are not nearly as mathe-
matically elegant and precise as the other indicators mentioned previously, we will then have a better attitude

toward their use. If, however, we use them to make defin-
itive or exclusive trading decisions, we can be tempted to
draw in lines under and over every little zigzag in price
movement, projecting ahead onto the right edge of the
chart myriad competing and conflicting lines. A chart too
full of trend and channel lines will only lead to indecision.

The following one-year chart of QQQQ (Figure
2.16) demonstrates well how you can get too carried away
with trend and channel lines. Just how are you supposed to
get a solid read of this chart?

It is best, therefore, to use trendlines only to give us
the big picture. When in doubt, remember KISS (Keep It
Simple, Stupid!). In other words, try to incorporate as
many highs and lows (price point touches) as possible as
you draw your lines and try to contain as much price action
as possible. Use trendlines only to focus on major trends
and channels, and, as we will see in greater detail later, they
will become very useful tools indeed.

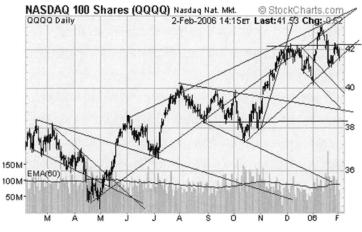

Figure 2.16   QQQQ with too many trendlines.

EYEBALLING THE CHARTS

Now that you have your charts set up, input each of the stocks on your primary watch list so that you can eyeball, or take a quick glance at, their daily charts. Don't worry if you do not yet have a watch list of stocks set up to monitor. In Chapter 9, I will show you how to set up an awesome watch list of the best stocks available for trend trading, and how to keep this list updated over time so that you always have only the best markets available to you. Here, I just want to introduce you to what will soon become a daily discipline for you: eyeballing the charts for current or developing setups.

Depending on which charting package you use, you can go through your watch lists, 10 at a time, page by page, or you can scroll through a drop-down menu of your watch list stocks and with the click of the mouse call up the daily chart for each one. Some charting packages will even let you set up a slide-show function that will scroll automatically through your lists for you. You simply sit back, watch, and take notes. It should be said that one advantage to saving your watch lists in a Web-based service rather than your charting package is that then if you, like me, trade from different computers, you will always have instant access to your watch lists through the Web. If your watch lists are saved only to your charting software, you will only be able to access your lists from the computer they are saved on unless you take the time to export and import the lists (a lot more easily said than done!).

Sometimes it is helpful to take your primary watch list and divide it into smaller lists. There are several ways to do this. You can, for example, divide by sector, by price, by index affiliation, or by some other scheme. I prefer to divide by sector, since I regularly monitor sector charts and like to key my trades off them. If, for example, I see the semiconductor sector flashing a fresh buy signal, I'll go to my semiconductor watch list and focus only on those stocks. The same is true for steel stocks, financials, Internets, China stocks, alternative energy plays, and so on. You can also make saved watch lists of those stocks that turn up on your special screens, as outlined later, but that have not yet given buy or sell signals. In any case, you will run through these watch lists at the end of each trading day, looking for new setups.

The eyeballing process is the bread and butter of trend traders. As technical analysts, our primary source of input is the price chart. The only way to receive that input is to lay your eyes on a number of them, day in and day out. Tune out the news, tune out CNBC, tune out the spam e-mail for "Hot stocks moving now!," tune out your buddy at the gym who has a hot stock tip. Your complete and entire investment discipline requires only that you eyeball the charts.

It is also important that before you begin eyeballing the charts on your primary watch list, you first ask yourself, "What do I expect the broader markets to do over the next few days?" If you expect a bullish period, then you will be eyeballing primarily for bullish setups. If you expect a bearish period, then you will be eyeballing primarily for bearish setups. If you are unsure about the general market direction, then you will be eyeballing for both bullish and bearish setups. (Don't worry if you don't yet know how to determine the general trend expectations of the broader markets. We will be covering that later.)

THE HERMENEUTICAL PROBLEM

I wrote my doctoral dissertation at Oxford on hermeneutics, the study of how the mind understands and applies the content of written texts. One of the things we can learn from this study is that no one reads texts in a vacuum. Whether we are reading the Bible or the nightly newspaper, we each bring our own experiences, biases, and personal preferences to what we are reading, and these in turn can influence how we understand and apply what we read.

A stock chart functions very much like a text. Like a text, a stock chart speaks to us about something we need to understand, but instead of using ordinary language, it uses price bars, candlesticks, moving averages, volume, and other technical indicators. Together, these are trying to tell us a story—a story about the underlying company's successes and failures and (if we listen very carefully) the future prospects of its publicly traded shares. But there is a problem in our ability to hear clearly what the chart wants to say to us, and it is a hermeneutical problem. The problem, simply put, is this: our prejudices (or our "prejudgments") get in the way.

Let's say, for example, that you plug into an Apple iPod at the gym, and you use an Apple Macintosh at the office, and you do your creative writing at Starbucks on an Apple MacBook. You are a big fan of Apple's products. Steve Jobs is your hero. You genuflect every time you pass the Cupertino exit on Highway 101. Okay, that's a bit much . . . but you get the point. You really like the company, think they can do no wrong, and believe their stock price is going to go "to da moon," as they say. These are prejudices, and they might prevent you from hearing what the stock chart wants to tell you.

Back in January of 2006, Apple (AAPL) could do no wrong. It was the darling of the street. Its stock price was hitting new all-time highs, up near $90 per share. Its products, especially the iPod, were seen everywhere. Rumors were flying about new products: an iPhone, an i-TV, and so on. However, the daily chart was trying to say something that only a few traders were willing to hear: not all was right with the way the shares were behaving. There were subtle sell signals forming in key indicators, like the MACD and stochastics. Sure enough, the next month the stock options backdating scandal hit the company and shares plummeted over the next two quarters to $50 (since then, of course, the iPhone did come out and AAPL shares ramped up to nearly $150!).

The moral of that story: ignore the hype, ignore the news, ignore your own prejudices, and just listen to what the chart is telling you. As much as possible, "bracket your prejudgments" (to use philosopher Edmund Husserl's phrase) and just tune in to the chart. As I like to tell my trading clients: price and volume—that is all you need to know to trade well.

Here is another example, but of a different kind. Broadwing (BWNG) is a company with a multifaceted footprint in the Internet sector. Through its subsidiaries,

the company provides data and Internet, broadband trans-
port, and voice communications services to several large
communications service providers. In late spring of 2006,
the company was hit with a string of events that sent its
earnings and its shares into a tailspin. Earnings announcements failed to meet Street expectations. There were unexpected changes in management. With really poor timing,
the company priced a large convertible debenture offering,
which further diluted shares. Price plummeted from a high
of $16.44 to a low of $8.26, for a loss of nearly 50 percent.
Former hedge fund manager Jim Cramer, on his hit CNBC
show *Mad Money*, called Broadwing a "dog" and told his
audience to sell it.

However, the chart of BWNG told us otherwise. As
price skidded to lows below $10 per share—a point that
normally takes a stock off the radar screen of professional
traders—certain indicators were pointing to the fact that
the stock was under accumulation. Momentum in the
latest sell-offs was waning, and the stock was ripe for a
turnaround. Bullish divergence was seen in several key indicators, telling us it was time to buy, not sell, shares.
Sure enough, three months later, shares had climbed to
$13 per share before they announced they were being
bought out by one of their competitors at a 20 percent
premium.

Again, the moral of the story is this: *just check the chart*.
If you don't like the chart, don't play the shares no matter
what the talking-head experts say. If the Street says sell but
the chart says buy, go with the chart. Always go with the
chart.

To read, understand, and apply what the chart is trying to tell you, you will have to face up to the hermeneutical problem. Again, this problem states that you have prejudices, biases, and personal preferences that may inhibit your hearing clearly what the chart has to say. Bracket them. Ignore them. Tell them to *shut up*! Just let the chart speak.

DEVELOPING A
TRADER'S MIND

T HERE are two types of traders who will buy this book, read it, and put one or more of its systems into practice in the markets. The first type will be successful, making money regularly from the markets, while the second type will consistently lose money until he or she finally gives up on trading altogether. The sad fact is that most traders will fall into the second category, and only a small percentage of those who buy this book will fall into the first category.

What is the difference between these two camps—between the successful trader and the losing trader? Believe it or not, the determining factor has nothing to do with education, nothing to do with innate intelligence, nothing to do with economic or business smarts. The difference is strictly psychological. No one can deduce a universal personality profile from the set of winning traders. Among successful traders, you will find introverts and extroverts, feeling types and thinking types, levelheaded automatons and passionate impulsives. But there are certain traits of *character* they hold in common. The trader who successfully puts these trading systems into practice is one who possesses all of the following:

f-discipline
ne ability to take responsibility
positive attitude toward success
- A keen understanding of risk
- The ability to maintain an open mind

The trader who unsuccessfully puts these trading systems into practice is more than likely lacking in one or more of the these qualities of character. Note that these are qualities of *character*, not *personality*. Attend any one of the three annual U.S. Trader's Expo symposia at which gather hundreds of wildly successful stock, options, and futures traders, and you will find every possible personality type represented (including some that probably should be on medication). But you will also find a narrow range of character traits—those listed here—that serve the trading career well.

In short, one's character or state of mind has a lot more to do with trading success than one's personality. I won't be saying too much about this topic, since there are many excellent resources available that can give you a much more detailed education. But what I have to say here might, in fact, be the most important part of this book. As the long-term successful trader you long to be, it is essential that you pay attention to the psychological side of your trading. You may have the world's most robust, most profitable trend-trading system at hand, but if fear, anxiety, panic, laziness, greed, or some other unhelpful mental state dominates your frame of thinking, you are much less likely to make that system work for you. Even 100 percent mechanical systems require a human hand to pull the trigger at each new signal. Like it or not, that hand is connected to a brain that makes it work.

CONTROLLING EMOTION

Contrary to popular opinion, there is not a specific emotional archetype that is ideal for the successful trader. Some portray the ideal trader as an emotionless robot, with ice for blood and a computer for a brain. But the truth is, highly profitable traders come in all sorts of emotional varieties. Think of Jim Cramer, the screaming, saliva-spewing host of CNBC's popular *Mad Money* show. Cramer is anything but emotionless, and by most accounts (including his own) his turn as a hedge fund manager was very successful. No, it's really not essential to trading that you curb your emotional enthusiasm and trade like a machine. Indeed, I believe that a passionate feeling for the markets, a "fire in the belly," is a real plus for the trader. What else is going to keep you coming back day after day to the tedious, often boring research that needs to be done? What else will get you back in the game after a losing streak?

What is essential is not rooting out all emotion while you are trading—an impossible task, in any case—but managing your emotions as they arise. When emotions cause impulsive trading, trading against the plan, trading against your best instincts, experience, and education, they are problematic. Any emotional state that undermines confidence in your edge as a trader will pose serious obstacles to your success. With the trading systems outlined in this book, you now have your edge on the markets. But that edge is worthless if it is not managed appropriately. As Ed

Seykota, the great futures trader, likes to say (and I para-phrase), trading is mostly about numbers, but once you've mastered the numbers, it's all about psychology.

The primary cause of failure in trading is not a bad trading system but bad trading psychology. Good trading psychology can best be defined as any mental condition that allows you enough confidence in your trading and money management strategies to hang on to your winners and cut short your losers. The first act, hanging on to winners, requires the trader to possess a state of mind that is comfortable with success and that avoids self-sabotage. The latter act, keeping losses small, requires a hard-nosed realism, an appreciation for risk, a mind open to the possibility that you are wrong, and the self-discipline to stick with prede-termined exit rules.

Developing this kind of winning trading attitude is no small task. Fortunately, there are several excellent resources available that have helped thousands of traders do just that. The first book I recommend is Mark Douglas's best-selling *Trading in the Zone*. I believe this to be the best resource currently available for helping traders develop the right attitude toward the markets they are trading. Douglas is president of Trading Behavior Dynamics, Inc., which develops seminars on trading psychology for brokerages, banks, and money managers. Douglas emphasizes that having a healthy respect for risk, a willingness to think in terms of probabilities instead of certainties, and an open mind toward whatever market expectations you may have are essential ingredients in the winner's mindset.

Douglas has conveniently included a trader's person-ality inventory test (it is better termed a "character inventory" test) in his book. Once this test is assessed, you will have a clear idea where you might be stuck emotionally and in terms of your core beliefs—that is, the test uncovers those specific mental attitudes that are the cause of so much trading failure. Douglas is convinced that as you align your core beliefs as a trader with what can rightly be expected from the markets over time, you will have the mental apparatus in place to take just about any trading system to the heights of success.

Here is how Douglas himself describes the essence of his work in *Trading in the Zone:*

> As long as you are susceptible to the kinds of errors that are the result of rationalizing, justifying, hesitating, hoping, and jumping the gun, you will not be able to trust yourself. If you can't trust yourself to be objective and to always act in your own best interests, achieving consistent results will be next to impossible. . . . The irony is that, when you have the appropriate attitude, when you have acquired a "trader's mind-set" and can remain confident in the face of constant uncertainty, trading will be as easy and simple as you probably thought it was when you first started out. So, what is the solution? You will need to learn how to adjust your attitudes and beliefs about trading in such a way that you can trade without the slightest bit of fear, but at the same time keep a framework in place that does not allow you to become reckless. That's exactly what this book is designed to teach you (Douglas, p. 15).

A second resource I can recommend is the longer, more complex work of Van K. Tharp, entitled *Trade Your Way to Financial Freedom*. Despite the title, Tharp's book does not outline a specific set of trading systems you can use to trade for a living. Instead, Tharp focuses on what it takes—mentally, emotionally, philosophically—to develop, trade, and stick with your own trading methodology. His essential point is that trading systems need to be matched to trading temperaments, so the better you can understand what kind of person you are, the better the trader you will be.

In a chapter Tharp admits to be "the most difficult to understand," the author outlines six variables that must be taken into account in any winning trading system: reliability, profit-to-loss ratio, transaction costs, trade frequency, initial account size, and position sizing. Tharp carefully outlines the importance of each of these variables, then relates them to the concept of *expectancy*, or what sort of returns you can reasonably expect a trading system to produce over time. As these variables change within a particular trading strategy, so will what can be expected of the strategy in terms of its returns. Consequently, with a simple tweaking of these variables, you can work toward a customized optimization of your trading system based on your particular trading psychology and objectives.

Tharp has over 20 years' experience working with individual and institutional traders as a consultant for the development of trading systems. He also manages a company, the International Institute of Trading Mastery, Inc., that produces home seminars on systems development and testing. Tharp's Web site (www.iitm.com) contains a wealth of resources for traders, including a free trading personality test and simulated trading game. Tharp nicely summarizes his trading philosophy in these words taken from the conclusion to *Trade Your Way to Financial Freedom*:

> First, you cannot trade the markets—you can only trade your beliefs about the market. As a result, it is important for you to determine exactly what those beliefs are. Second, certain key beliefs, which have nothing to do with the market, will determine your success in the markets. Those are your beliefs about yourself. What do you think you are capable of doing? Is trading for success important to you? How worthy of success do you believe yourself to be? Weak beliefs about yourself can undermine trading with a great system (Tharp, pp. 322–323).

VALUES-BASED TRADING

The last resource I'd like to mention is a book that makes no mention of trading but has tremendous application to cultivating a healthy trading psychology. The book made its appearance in late 2005 and quickly rose to the top of the *New York Times* best-seller list. Early in 2006 the author was interviewed by *Time* magazine.* Needless to say, the impact of the book has been tremendous. Not only have the author's teachings been taken up by the general

---

* John Cloud, "Happiness Isn't Normal," *Time*, February 13, 2006. Much of the description of Acceptance and Commitment Therapy in what follows is taken from this article.

public, they have also caused an important reassessment—though not without debate—of traditional psychological therapies.

The book is provocatively titled *Get Out of Your Mind and Into Your Life*. Its author, Steven Hayes, is a professor of psychology at the University of Nevada—Reno. After suffering from a series of unexpected panic attacks—so severe that he couldn't properly teach his classes—Hayes pursued research into various models of therapy designed to overcome depression and anxiety. It seemed natural that Hayes, as former president of the Association of Behavioral and Cognitive Therapies, would turn to these dominant schools of psychology to treat himself. But he soon found that neither behavioral nor cognitive modification could effectively treat his particular illness. Hayes then began to incorporate the Eastern practice of mindfulness into his therapy, with positive results. To this he also added the discipline of consciously committing himself, not to what his emotions dictated, but to the values that matter most to him, to his personal convictions and beliefs. And with this amalgam came his healing—and a new form of psychological therapy as well.

What Hayes had discovered during his experiments in self-healing came to be called Acceptance and Commitment Therapy (ACT). Today ACT stands alongside the psychoanalytical, behavioral, and cognitive schools of therapy as the next big wave in psychotherapeutic practice. ACT has generated an impressive pedigree of clinical support, with healing claims for everything from addictions to schizophrenia. Skeptics dismiss it as a passing fad, but there is a growing contingent of professional counselors who are embracing its primary mantra: *Accept who you are and commit yourself to who you want to become.*

So how does ACT work, and of what use is it to trading? In short—you will have to read *Get Out of Your Mind* for the full version—ACT proposes that whenever we have a negative thought, instead of deprogramming it as cognitive therapy suggests, we should embrace it. We are to acknowledge the thought with attention and mindfulness, for as we do so, Hayes insists, we distance ourselves from the thought and therefore negate its power. So, for example, instead of saying, "I am depressed," we are to say, "I am having the thought that I'm depressed." In this way the thought becomes something I *have* rather than something I *am*. As such, it is much more easily discarded.

The second step in ACT, then, is to commit yourself to what you most value. Having mindfully defused the power of the negative thought, you must then just step out in faith into what is believed to be the right course of action, even if your emotions are not supportive. To facilitate this commitment, Hayes recommends spending quality time outlining your personal philosophy (or philosophies) of life, what you value most highly, what you want to accomplish before dying, and so on. This then gives you a kind of road map to follow during the darker times.

I am incredibly excited about the possibility of applying this new therapy to trading. Here is how I envision ACT being used by the active trader: imagine that every time you have a negative thought about your trading, you were also able to detach yourself from, and thus defuse, the thought before it affected your trading decisions. I know how negative the trader's mind can be at times. I have personally experienced the waves of regret, fear, anxiety, and anger that come with every tick of the tape when it goes against your position. How helpful would it be if you could find a way to negate these emotional waves, and thus free yourself to follow your system strictly and profitably!

Now imagine that you have written down somewhere near your trading station a list of your commitments as a trader. As for me, I have a number of bright yellow sticky notes pasted to my monitor with pithy, bold, all-caps statements on them. These include:

- Trade only your own picks!
- Never average down!
- Let winners run!
- Cut losses short!
- No impulse buys or sells!

You can probably guess that behind each of these statements lies a terribly embarrassing, losing trade that motivated me in absolute horror to write out a maxim and slap it to the monitor. You can also likely imagine that behind each of these commitment statements lies a particular value, something that I highly honor and desire as a trader. My own list of trading values looks something like this:

- Your trading systems are sound and profitable.
- You are in control of your impulses.
- Trade with integrity at all times.
- Trade responsibly for your family's financial future.

- Trading is only a means to an end.
- Profits come with the system, not with hunches.

Now imagine that these and other trading values were to govern my every trading decision—how much better a trader I would be! Thus, regardless of what I am feeling emotionally, as I detach myself from those impulsive feelings that so often foul up my trading decisions I am free to follow a structured road map of my own design, hammered out by the hard-won experience of years of trading. This is the promise of ACT when applied to trading: its tools help me to clear and focus my mind so that I can commit myself to following my system despite how I'm feeling about a particular trade.

So what if you don't have a set of trading rules or values for yourself? What if you are not sure what personal psychological frame of thinking is most suited to active trading? This is where the Douglas and Tharp books are helpful. Together, they will provide for you that emotional blueprint you need to follow as you construct your trader's mind.

CHAPTER 4

THE 10 HABITS OF HIGHLY SUCCESSFUL TRADERS

BACK in the winter of 2003 I held an online seminar for several hundred of our clients, most of whom were relatively new to trading. In two grueling four-hour sessions we covered the basics of chart reading, candlesticks, and trend trading. I also included a full explanation of two never-before-taught trend trading setups that I had been working on the previous year. During the question-and-answer period, however, I was surprised to find that most of the concerns of the audience had little to do with the logistics of trend trading and more to do with the specific details of my trading approach. In order to answer those questions as precisely as possible, I promised my clients that I would write up my trading rules and send them each a copy.

The following list is a replica of that original set of rules I sent my clients. None of the rules have changed since then, though some of their applications have gotten a bit more sophisticated. As always with trading, there are exceptions allowed, as dictated by current market conditions.

THE 10 HABITS OF HIGHLY SUCCESSFUL TRADERS

1. *Follow the Rule of Three.* There are many indicators a technical analyst uses to determine whether or not to take a particular trade. There are patterns the price bars make on the chart; there are moving averages of price; there are various momentum and overbought/oversold indicators as well. Together, these form a pictorial description of where a stock's current price is, relative to its price history. My Rule of Three says that I will not enter any trade unless I can carefully articulate three reasons from among my list of technical indicators for doing so. Three is the minimum, and more is better. So often young traders take a trade for only one reason: a double bottom, for example, or overbought stochastics. These indicators need to be confirmed by others working in tandem. Conflicting indicators signal a confused market. We don't want that. We want to enter on conviction, not confusion. So always wait until you can satisfy the Rule of Three (at least). Remember, trading is a game of probabilities, and you should always stack the odds in your favor.

2. *Keep losses small.* Bernard Baruch, the great Wall Street speculator from the turn of the last century, once said, "Even being right three or four times out of ten should yield a person a fortune if he has the sense to cut his losses quickly." Baruch was right. It is important to keep losses to a minimum, as most large losses started out as small ones, and large losses can end your trading permanently. Normally, we keep our losses small by setting stop-losses on all open trades. We do this on all trades that we are not monitoring on a minute-by-minute basis; otherwise, we will keep a mental stop in place and exit the position once that price level is violated. Remember Warren Buffett's Rule #1: "Don't Lose Money!" Buffett also made a second rule: "Don't forget Rule #1!" So take a tip from the world's greatest investor and always strive to keep your losses small.

3. *Adjust stops and targets at the end of the day.* At the end of each trading day, on a high-watermark basis, adjust your stop-loss or target price as needed. Here "high water mark" means you adjust either the stop or target only if the closing price sets a new high or low from the point of entry. This is how it works: raise your stop-loss price at each new closing high since entry (or new low if the trade is a short). And if you are using a target price as an exit, lower your target price at each new low if the trade goes against you (or raise at each new high if short). Don't get complacent with your trades. Monitor them each day at least once near the close, and adjust your stops and targets accordingly. It is also a good idea to take off your stops overnight to avoid the wide fluctuations of after-hours trading. But do keep your target orders in place. I like to break down my target limit order into smaller bits and set them one penny apart. Occasionally, one or more of these get filled overnight in the sort of erratic, widely ranging trading that characterizes the after-hours market.

4. *Keep commissions low.* Use a discount broker of your choice that charges a maximum of $10 per trade. There are several online brokers (OLBs) that charge as little as, or even less than, $0.01 per share per trade. You should *not* be paying more than this. The qualitative differences between an OLB charging $30 per trade and one charging $1 per trade are minimal at best. Both will offer you fast fills, occasional price improvement between the spread, frills like automatically trailing stops, boxing and basket orders, and the ability to trade funds, options, and futures. Why pay a premium for a brand name? Remember, commissions are part of your overhead costs—and when running any business, the lower you can keep your overhead costs, the more profits you get to take to the bank!

5. *Amateurs at the open, pros at the close.* What this familiar trading adage means is that, in general, the well-funded institutional traders often fade (or trade against) the morning momentum, happily handing shares to anxious amateurs, before going off to gorge themselves on a high-fat lunch. When they get back to their desks around 2:30 p.m. EST, they fully expect to be able to pick up the same shares at a better price. They are usually right. That's why they are professionals. They get paid to be right about things like that. So if you must trade in the morning, be sure to ease into your trades in smaller portions. Yes, you might miss out on some nice moves, but in the long run you will save yourself money. Even better: look to enter your trades within the last two hours of trading. In that way you are more likely to be in sync with the larger and more determinative moves caused by professional trading.

6. *Know the general market trend, and trade accordingly.* This is more easily said than done, but it is absolutely essential to successful trend trading. You need to know each day what kind of market you are currently trading in. We will say more about this in Chapter 5. Here the general rule can be stated that the type of market we are in will determine the type of trade you put on. There are five general types of market trends: weak uptrend, strong uptrend, weak downtrend, strong downtrend, and range-bound. In weak uptrends and downtrends, you should focus on continuation plays; in strong uptrends and downtrends, you should focus on breakout plays; and in range-bound markets, you should look for reversal setups. Again, these terms will be discussed in the next chapter.

You should also ask whether the current trend or range-bound condition is relatively new or relatively old. The longer a market persists in its current condition (uptrend, downtrend, or range-bound), the shorter your time frame should be for new positions. For example, if we are in the early weeks of a new bull market, you should feel comfortable setting a higher target on your long positions. But if you are long during an overbought market (an older bull market), you should aim to take quick profits when given. One quick and easy way to determine the kind of market we are in is to apply the 50-day moving average of closing prices to a chart of the S&P 500. Then simply look at the slope. Is its slope upward (weakly or strongly), downward (weakly or strongly), or flat (range-bound)? Has it been this way for a while (prolonged), or did it just turn (new)? And so on.

*7. **Write down every trade.*** We keep track of so many other things in life—the checks we write, the groceries we need, the donations to charity we make, our golf scores, the last time we changed the oil in the car—but how many of us write down the details of every trade we make? In reading the *Market Wizards* books by Jack Schwager (which

I highly recommend, by the way), you learn that nearly all of the wizards keep trading journals. I suggest you do the same. Make a spreadsheet that records the date of each trade entry and exit, the symbol of the market traded, the price of your entry and exit, the size of the trade, the profit or loss, a running total of profits/losses, and a comment section where you describe as specifically as possible why you entered and exited the trade. If you are adept at working with spreadsheets, you can even program columns to keep track of your stop-losses, target prices, and position size.

Analyze these trades at the end of each month. Are you consistently losing with one particular setup? Are your breakout plays working better than your reversal plays? Are your stops set too tight? Use this journal to learn about your weaknesses as a trader. Awareness of those weaknesses should soon lead to overcoming them. If you have any trouble setting up your spreadsheet, e-mail me at support@befriendthetrend.com, and my staff will be happy to send you the one I use.

8. *Never average down on a losing position.* Let's say you buy a stock, expecting it to take off like a rocket, and instead it drops like a rock. What do you do? Answer: you do nothing. You stick with your plan. You keep your stop-loss in place, lower your target at the end of the day, and wait patiently. Do not buy more shares at a lower price to make your average cost lower. That is a loser's game. You already own shares at that price; why buy more? Why throw good money after bad? Just sit on your hands and let the market do what it wants. Now the one exception to this rule is when you are positioning yourself into a trade and on your entry day you take advantage of a small dip in share price. But in this case you must still be favorable toward the chart, far away from your stop price, and price is showing signs of recovering from its slight dip.

9. *Never overtrade.* You know the feeling: you've closed out all your overnight trades for a tidy profit and you say to yourself, hey, I'm on a winning streak, let's take advantage of it. So you put on a few more trades. But these don't go well, and now you are back to breakeven. You want those morning profits back, so you put on a few more trades, only now you go with the e-minis or a few, deep in-the-money options to leverage your position. These don't go well either, and you close the day with a loss. Or perhaps you start the day by closing out losing positions, and you overtrade to try to get the money back, only to deepen your losses on the day. This is the obsessive-compulsive disorder known as *overtrading*. It is a problem familiar to all traders and is rooted in deep-seated feelings of fear and greed.

The best way to overcome this behavior is to set limits on yourself: when you reach a certain profit point during the day, either reduce your position size or just quit. Better yet, when you reach a certain number of trades during the day, just quit. Reward yourself then for your disciplined behavior: go sit by the pool, read a good book, take a bike ride in the woods—just do something nice to reinforce this discipline until it becomes a habit.

10. *Give at least 10 percent of all trading earnings to charity.* The children of John D. Rockefeller were taught five basic rules regarding money: (a) work for all you get, (b) give away the first 10 percent, (c) invest the next 10 percent, (d) live on the rest, (e) and account for every penny. The Rockefellers believed that giving away their money was essential to their wealth. And so should you. The secret is that money multiplies fastest when it's divided. It's all God's money, in any case. We are merely temporary stewards of a small portion of God's abundance. And when this portion is shared freely with those less fortunate, we prime the economic pump of the universe.

I encourage you to establish a legacy that will outlive you. Plant money trees from which others will harvest the fruit. Ultimately, the only purpose for having wealth is to help others less fortunate. Wealth shared is true wealth indeed. The way I see it, God in His grace gave me the undeserved talent to make money by simply sitting in front of a computer and clicking a mouse every now and then. As a result of that gift, we as a family have been able to travel the world, build a large home, and enjoy some of the finer things in life. The least I can do is give a healthy portion of the fruits of that gift back to God's work in the world.

TREND-TRADING
BASICS

CHAPTER 5

WHAT IS TREND
TRADING?

TREND trading is a form of trading that seeks to maximize trading profits and minimize risk by entering and exiting strategic price chart setups. While the trend-trading systems outlined here can be applied to any time frame—from multimonth position trades to multiminute day trades—most trend trades are held from 3 to 30 trading days. It is called *trend* trading because it seeks to enter already established trends (for the most part) and ride them as they swing up or down to new highs or lows. But before we further define what trend trading is, let's first separate the idea from what it is not.

WHAT TREND TRADING IS NOT

Trend Trading Is Not
Buy-and-Hold Investing

Buy-and-hold investing involves the fundamental or economic analysis of market cycles, business sectors, and individual companies with the intent of buying solid companies, or funds of such companies, when valuations are attractive or when growth prospects are strong, or, ideally, both. The aim of this strategy is to realize long-term capital gains with a minimum of portfolio turnover. Buy-and-hold investors are not traders. They normally pay little attention to even the basics of technical analysis. A price chart trend either up or down matters little to them. What matters instead is, in Warren Buffett's terms, "buying a great company at a fair price." The holding time of a buy-and-hold position is usually measured in years. In some cases buy-and-hold investments can last a lifetime.

Trend Trading Is Not Position Trading

Position traders are indeed traders inasmuch as they normally rely on the technical analysis of price charts rather than the fundamental analysis of companies. Rather than positioning themselves within already established trends, however, their aim is to get in on the beginning of new trends, or even in anticipation of a trend prior to its beginning. In other words, position traders like to buy bottoms and sell tops, two things that trend traders are forbidden to do except in a very limited sense (e.g., buying the bottom of a dip to support in an established uptrend). Compared to trend trading, position trading requires quite a bit more patience. Position trades are normally measured in months and can last a year or longer. The primary chart of the position trader is the weekly chart, with the daily chart being used to time entries and exits. If a position trade is entered too soon, the trader is forced to sit through sometimes lengthy drawdowns.

Trend Trading Is Not Overnight Trading

The overnight trader is someone who relies on technical analysis and tape-reading skills, along with (sometimes) intraday news breaks, to take a quick two-day position in a stock. The overnight trader normally enters the position late in the trading day and sells before the close of the day following. The overnight trader's aim is to capture three phases of movement: the afternoon run, the overnight gap, and the next-day continuation. This is a very profitable form of trading for someone with sound trading strategies and a keen understanding of what prompts a stock's momentum, but it can be very time consuming, and trading the exit requires as much focused attention as day trading. While trend-trading skills can be used in overnight trading, it is a multifaceted discipline and thus goes beyond the normal range of trend trading.

Trend Trading Is Not Scalping

Scalping is a form of day trading inasmuch as positions are held for only one trading day and all positions are exited prior to or at the close of the trading day. As a day trader, a scalper always goes home *flat* (completely in cash) at the end of each trading session, with no open positions held overnight. But scalping differs from ordinary day trading (which can be a subspecies of trend trading) in that positions are normally held for only a few seconds, or at most a few minutes. And while day traders usually rely on their chart-reading skills, scalpers play only on the tape. They isolate the stocks that are moving sharply that day—

usually in response to unexpected news, an earnings announcement, an upgrade or downgrade, or the like—and scrutinize the tape (Level I and II quotes) for opportunistic, quick-turn in-and-out trades. Scalpers put on lots of trades each day, sometimes in the hundreds, with the aim to make only a small profit on each (a *scalp*). These small profits are leveraged into larger profits by increasing both the volume of trades and the position size. Because scalpers make little reference to price charts, they are technically not trend traders.

WHAT TREND TRADING IS

In terms of time frame, trend trading occupies the range of holding periods between the multimonth position trader at the one extreme and the multisecond scalper at the other. The primary aim of the trend trader is to capture the bulk of major moves in trending stocks, entering after the trend has begun and normally exiting before the trend concludes. Trend traders use the price chart in a time frame that best fits their intended holding period. If the trend-trading system is applied to swing trading (see later discussion), for example, then the trade will likely be held from 5 to 30 trading days. In swing trading, the daily chart is used primarily. But the trend-trading systems outlined here can also be used for day-trading purposes, in which case an intraday chart like the five-minute period is most commonly used and the position held for only minutes or a few hours at most.

  Thus, it is important to think of trend trading as a set

of trading systems and not a trading style. Your particular trading style (position trader, swing trader, day trader, etc.) has to be determined by, among other things, your trading objectives, the limits of your time, your temperament and skills (e.g., unless you have quick reflexes, don't even think about scalping), and your income expectations. Further clarification of the different types of trading styles can be found later in this chapter. (Note that only swing trading and day trading, as defined here, are forms of trend trading.)

Buy-and-Hold Investing
- *Aim:* Long-term capital gains
- *Style:* Fundamental analysis of sectors and companies
- *Holding time:* One year or longer
- *Time investment:* A few hours each month
- *Turnover rate:* One to five trades per year
- *Commission costs:* Minimal
- *Expected annual return:* A gain of 15 percent or more

Position Trading
- *Aim:* Quarterly income
- *Style:* Technical analysis of weekly/daily charts
- *Holding time:* Three to six months
- *Time investment:* A few hours each week
- *Turnover rate:* One to five trades per quarter
- *Commission costs:* Moderately low
- *Expected annual return:* A gain of 25 percent or more

Swing Trading—(Can Be a Form of Trend Trading)

- *Aim:* Monthly income
- *Style:* Technical analysis of daily/hourly charts
- *Holding time:* Five to thirty trading days
- *Time investment:* One to three hours each day
- *Turnover rate:* Five to fifteen trades per month
- *Commission costs:* Moderately high
- *Expected annual return:* A gain of 40 percent or more

Overnight Trading

- *Aim:* Weekly income
- *Style:* Technical analysis of daily/hourly charts
- *Holding time:* Two days maximum
- *Time investment:* Six to eight hours each day
- *Turnover rate:* Two to five trades per day
- *Commission costs:* Moderately high
- *Expected annual return:* A gain of 50 percent or more

Day Trading (Can Be a Form of Trend Trading)

- *Aim:* Daily income
- *Style:* Technical analysis of intraday charts
- *Holding time:* Minutes to hours, one day maximum
- *Time investment:* Eight to twelve hours each day
- *Turnover rate:* Five or more trades per day
- *Commission costs:* Very high
- *Expected annual return:* A gain of 60 percent or more

Scalping
- *Aim:* Daily income
- *Style:* Chasing momentum, tape reading
- *Holding time:* Seconds to minutes
- *Time investment:* Eight to twelve hours each day
- *Turnover rate:* Twenty or more trades per day
- *Commission costs:* Extremely high
- *Expected annual return:* A gain of 70 percent or more

ADVANTAGES OF TREND TRADING

The advantages of trend trading over other forms of trading are numerous. Obviously, the anticipated returns tend to be higher than what a buy-and-hold investor would expect, even over what position traders expect, making trend trading in either its longer-term (swing trading) or shorter-term (day-trading) forms an ideal way to trade for a living. If you do not hold a day job and have 8 to 10 hours of free time each day—not to mention the inclination to spend that time sitting in front of a computer screen clicking a mouse—then day trading may be the ideal way to transform the trend-trading techniques outlined in this book into a very profitable business. If you don't have that much spare time or would rather be doing other things than squinting at pixels all day, then swing trading using the trend-trading strategies we outline here may be the ideal way to trade for a living.

Perhaps more important, trend trading does not require the same level of expertise that sound buy-and-holders need to turn a reasonable profit year after year. No doubt about it, phenomenal wealth can be attained through long-term investing—but it takes a lot of hard work, a lot of time, and a bit of luck as well. One of the world's wealthiest men, Warren Buffett, is the epitome of the intelligent, successful long-term investor, buying sound companies at steeply discounted prices. But Buffett works very hard at what he does. He knows the businesses he buys inside and out. He lunches with the company's executives; he interviews middle management; he visits the company's manufacturing plants and supply chains; he pores night and day over oodles of bottom-line information—all before committing one dime of his hard-earned cash to a new investment. Even then, there is little guarantee of success. While Buffett is truly an investing genius, his returns over the past 10 years have averaged only a little over 6 percent annually.

As a trend trader, do you have to work as hard as Warren Buffett? No! You simply take one of the systems taught in these pages, go over a few charts each night, click the mouse a few times in the morning, and you are all set to make a decent living.

Moreover, buy-and-hold investors, and to a lesser extent position traders, must have a great deal of patience. They have to wait months, if not years, for the fruits of their labor to become evident. Not so with trend trading. This is what makes trend trading so ideal for those who want to trade for a living. Stock market trends are fairly short-lived phenomena. Up to 80 percent of the time, stocks move sideways; they run in trends only about 20 percent of the time. To follow trend-trading techniques is to move in and out of stocks on a weekly (for swing traders) or hourly (for day traders) basis. Thus, the payoff for your efforts is more immediately seen.

This makes trend-trading techniques ideal for setting up trading as a primary source of your income. If you apply trend-trading systems to swing trading, say, your income can be made available on a monthly basis due to the relatively high turnover rate. This allows the trend trader to trade two weeks for income to pay the monthly bills and then two more weeks to compound the trading account. With day trading, the income is available even more frequently. What I do as manager of our Befriend the Trend Fund is combine the two: swing trading for larger moves with day trading to exploit intraday moves.

It needs to be said, of course, that like all forms of trading, trend trading is susceptible to market fluctuations and cycles. While you can trend-trade for a living, you need to be very careful to set aside funds during the good periods in order to have money available to pay the bills during the lean periods. Like any form of trading or investing, there certainly will be lean periods.

Another advantage to trend trading is that when properly executed, trend-trading strategies of the type taught here will yield much less risk than longer-term strategies. Long-term investors are forced to ride bear markets into the ground, anxiously watching their net worth slip away as the indexes grind down day after day. But trend traders have the freedom to simply exit losing trades quickly and step aside. Or they can use one of the strategies outlined here that are designed especially for bear markets to play on the short side and thus make money while the investing world suffers a drawdown.

Finally, to trend-trade well, you needn't worry about . . .

- Poring over financial statements like buy-and-hold investors
- Catching precise market tops and bottoms like position traders
- Seeing the bulk of your profits evaporate on overnight gaps that go against you like overnight traders
- Learning the sophisticated nuances of Level II and other tape-reading devices like scalpers

In short, trend trading provides the greatest amount of return for the least amount of work of any trading style. So, let's get started *trend trading for a living*!

SETTING UP YOUR
WATCH LISTS

THERE are over 10,000 listed and over-the-counter stocks available for trading daily—and the list grows every week. It is impossible to monitor the whole universe of trading vehicles on a daily basis. So the logical thing to do, and what trend traders must do before they do anything else, is create and regularly update watch lists of stocks that meet certain criteria. It is from these watch lists that we will select most of the stocks we use for trend trading.

In order to create a watch list, we will need to screen out those stocks that are unsuitable for trend trading. Some charting services will offer special screening tools for subscribers, but for our purposes the free stock screeners offered by Yahoo! Finance are sufficient. Note that Yahoo! Finance offers two free screening tools: a basic service and a more advanced one. You should use the more advanced tool, since the basic screener does not allow for screening by volume. Fee-based screening can be found at Stockcharts.com and at IQCharts; a subscription to either service includes screening and scanning tools as part of the package. I can also recommend the screening tool in OmniTrader from Nirvana Systems. It runs very slowly and thus is not suitable for frequent use, but it otherwise is a very powerful resource.

YOUR PRIMARY WATCH LIST

I recommend setting up a list of possible trend-trading candidates by screening for the following three criteria: price, average volume, and beta (a function of stock volatility relative to the broader market). There are usually lots of other options available in screening packages—things such as price/earnings ratios, quarterly growth trends, debt/equity ratios, and often, too, a variety of technical variables. Just ignore them for now. Subsequent chapters outline ways to harness the full power of your screening tool to find great trend-trading setups. To set up your primary watch lists all you need are the three variables mentioned.

In screening for *price*, we want to weed out stocks that are either too low in price (i.e., we want to avoid "penny stocks") or too high in price. In screening for *volume*, we want to avoid thinly traded stocks. In screening for *beta*, we want to eliminate slow-moving and nontrending stocks. Specifically, I recommend screening per the following settings:

- *Price:* between $10 and $100
- *Average daily volume:* greater than 500,000
- *Beta:* greater than 2.0 (at least twice as volatile as the S&P 500)

This screen should return at least 50 stocks, and most of the time it will yield well over that. But in certain market conditions you may get less than 50 hits, in which case it may be necessary to fiddle a bit with the numbers. In a breakaway bull market of the kind we saw in the late 1990s, for example, we may need to raise our maximum stock price to capture the higher-priced big movers. In certain markets you are forced to pay up for quality, and when it comes to stocks, that is nearly always a wise thing to do. Sometimes the market goes into a quiet period without much movement, in which case we may not be able to find many stocks trading at a 2.0 beta. In that case, the figure may need to be lowered a bit.

Traders with smaller accounts may want to focus only on lower-priced stocks. In this case, you can change the price screen to something like $5 to $50, or whatever is most suitable. Traders with larger accounts and options traders who are looking for daily multipoint swings may want to raise the price range accordingly. At Befriendthetrend.com we keep two separate watch lists to serve our two most popular newsletters: one designed for smaller account traders (stocks priced $5 to $15) and one for larger account traders (stocks priced $15 and up). Keeping two separate lists like this gives me a very interesting bit of market information: I know we are in a bull market when I have too many stocks showing up in the higher-priced screen and too few in the lower-priced screen—and vice versa for bear markets.

Regarding volume, it is important to note that we want to screen for *average daily volume*, not single-day volume. This avoids stocks that have a one-day high-volume event but which on average are too thinly traded to suit our purposes. It bears repeating that in no case should the average volume figure be lowered below 500,000 daily shares. Liquidity means stability, stability means lowered risk, and lowered risk means greater profits in the long run; thus, liquidity is an essential element in building a long-term trading career.

Once this screen returns a list of stocks, *sort the list by order of decreasing beta*. To make your primary watch list, take the first 50 stocks on that list, that is, the top 50 stocks ranked by order of decreasing beta. These are the stocks you are going to monitor daily for trading setups. Don't select more than 50, because in certain market conditions you will register too many setups to trade. Nor should you limit your list to less than 50, because in nontrending markets you may not have any setups at all.

Once you have your list of 50 stocks, write these into your charting software and save them as a focus list. As an alternative, you can input the list into the Candleglance feature on Stockscharts.com. This feature gives you 10 thumbnail charts per Web page, and includes the 20- and 50-period moving averages and one technical indicator of your choice on each chart. Figures 6.1 through 6.6 represent the six top high-beta, liquid stocks priced between $10 and $100 as screened on September 21, 2007 (note: my initial screen returned 247 stocks, which is typical of bull markets like the one we are in now). I've added the CCI indicator and set the charts at the two-month time period (this also is variable). This is what Candleglance charts look like once you have set them up.

Another site I like for keeping watch lists is Clear station.com, which allows you to keep an infinite number of lists for free. If you input your list of stocks into Clearstation—to do this you will have to register with the

Figure 6.1   CRM two-month chart with CCI and 20/50 MAs.

Figure 6.2   AKS two-month chart with CCI and 20/50 MAs.

Figure 6.3   LMC two-month chart with CCI and 20/50 MAs.

Figure 6.4 RMBS two-month chart with CCI and 20/50 MAs.

Figure 6.5 JOYG two-month chart with CCI and 20/50 MAs.

Figure 6.6 BZH two-month chart with CCI and 20/50 MAs.

site—not only will you get thumbnail charts with moving averages, stochastics, and MACD, you will also get daily updates on which of your stocks have had upgrades or downgrades, are expecting earnings, and have just triggered certain technical buy and sell signals. An advantage of the Clearstation watch lists is that you only need to bookmark one page to access all your charts; with Stockcharts' Candleglance feature you have to bookmark one page for each 10 stocks on your list. A disadvantage is that Clearstation only offers bar charts, whereas Stockcharts uses the more informative candlestick chart as its default.

I use both these services because each offers a slightly different set of tools. I do prefer the watch list capacity at Stockcharts to that of Clearstation, since, as a subscriber, I have access to updates in real time (versus delayed time for Clearstation). In truth, both are ideal for sorting through dozens of stocks to find a shortlist of the charts you want to do further research on.

UPKEEP OF YOUR WATCH LIST

Now, with your watch list of the 50 most liquid and most volatile stocks set up, you have the set of charts you will monitor at the end of each trading day (or as a day trader, throughout the day). To trend-trade effectively you will need to become very familiar with these price charts. Forget the companies themselves, what they make, what service they offer, what their growth prospects are, and so on. All of that is now irrelevant to your purposes as a trend trader. Everything you need to know to trend-trade for a living is right there in the price chart; the rest is just noise.

After looking at their charts day after day, you will begin to develop a feel for how these stocks trade. As you train yourself in the trend-trading systems outlined in this book, you will learn to recognize points of support and resistance. You will be able to make notes of special trading opportunities as they set up on the charts (breakouts, breakdowns, consolidations, movements toward or away from major moving averages, etc.). You will be able to distinguish those that look like easy traders—that is, ones that make smooth turns, rarely gap up or down, and have a steady volume flow—from those that look more difficult. The more difficult stocks to trade tend to have sloppy, choppy price movements, wide overnight gaps, and huge intraday ranges. These you should delete from your watch list. You can replace them with stocks farther down the list of your original screening. Remember, trading is a business and these price charts are your employees. As a good boss, you should keep close tabs on them: fire the unproductive ones and replace them with more eager workers.

Your primary watch list will need to be updated once a month. To do this, simply repeat the same process: screen for price, volume, and beta; select the 50 highest beta stocks; then input these into your charting software. As you do your monthly updates you will find that the list does not change all that much over time. The same great trading vehicles keep getting screened out from among the masses. But in most market conditions you should be replacing about half a dozen stocks at each new screening. Keep track of these new additions, because you will now need to become just as familiar with them as you were with those they replaced. Also, whenever a company is bought out or has a horrible news event, it is best to delete it from your watch list. Large, multipoint gaps either up or down tend to make for messy trading in the weeks and months going forward.

In addition to this primary list of trading stocks, you should add, on a daily basis, a few stocks that are screened for special trading setups. These setups are described later. You can add these stocks to those you have chosen from your primary watch list, or you can do what I do: make separate watch lists for each special setup screen.

One last word on updating your watch lists: if you choose to use Stockcharts.com for keeping your watch lists, you have the advantage of moving the results of your special setup screens directly into your watch lists with a single click of the mouse. Since you will eventually be screening for up to 10 setups—which means potentially having 10 different watch lists in addition to your primary list—this can prove to be a valuable timesaving option.

CHAPTER 7

DETERMINING
GENERAL MARKET
DIRECTION

THE art of applying technical analysis to your watch lists and then selecting which stocks to trade is a chart-specific exercise. This is to say, your primary point of reference is the stock's price chart itself. All you need to know to make profitable predictions about a stock's future price movement are the patterns of its past price movements as recorded on the stock's daily chart. This means that, with the tools of technical analysis in your trading arsenal, you do *not* need to:

- Watch every minute of CNBC or Bloomberg Television
- Pore through hundreds of profit and loss statements—*boring*!
- Track prior quarters for earnings and revenue growth
- Worry about things like price/earnings ratios and debt/equity ratios
- Monitor every news dispatch on Briefing.com or Reuters
- Keep track of gross domestic product (GDP), the

consumer price index (CPI), the producer price
index (PPI), housing starts, and employment data
- Hang on every syllable of the latest Federal
  Reserve announcement
- Anticipate mergers, buyouts, public offerings,
  splits, FDA approvals, and so on

Instead, all you need to do to trend-trade profitably with
technical analysis is to check the chart, find trends, enter
them after they start, and exit them when they end.

Having said that, there is one further bit of analysis
beyond the stock's price chart that you can do to add to the
likelihood that your trade will go in the intended direction.
It also involves applying technical analysis to a price chart,
but instead of the chart of the stock you intend to trade,
you will now be looking at the chart of the broader market. If you can correlate your trade as much as possible with
the general market's directionality and momentum, then
you will add significant percentage points to the probability that your trade will turn out a winner.

In his best-selling book *How to Make Money in Stocks*,
William O'Neil includes *market direction* as an important
part of his CAN-SLIM trading strategy (it is the "M" in
SLIM). O'Neil's strategy combines basic principles of fundamental analysis with an assessment of the price chart of
the Dow Jones Industrial Average. O'Neil rightly concludes
that to give your trades every chance of success, whenever
possible you should avoid two fundamental mistakes: going
long in a bear market and buying into the top of a market
run.

But O'Neil overstates the case when he says, "If you

are wrong about the direction of the broad general market, three out of four of your stocks will slump with the market averages and you will lose money" (O'Neil, p. 44). If you follow the systems I outline here, you will be able to make good money long in a bear market and short in a bull market.

The key to trend-trading success in any type of market is finding good charts. And there are always great charts that shine brightly during bear markets, just as there are many laggards that stink up the place during bull markets. Again, any robust technical system must be chart-specific: if directional movement is not happening in the daily chart of the stock, it doesn't matter what the general market is doing, your stock position is not likely to move.

Still, it is important to have a general sense of what type of market we are in: bull, bear, or range-bound. One reason this is important is not because our success is dependent on it, but because it makes our job a lot easier. It is much easier to find good long setups in a bull market than in a bear market. And you will have many more shorts to choose from in a bear market than in a bull market. So understanding the current market dynamic and playing it accordingly is really an exercise in efficiency. More important, perhaps, knowing and trading with the general market direction can put a few percentage points of probability on our side. Were we infallible chart readers, this would not matter. But the fact that bull markets tend to cause more stocks to go up than down, and bear markets cause more stocks to go down than up, means that getting on the side of the general market direction can help cover a multitude of chart-reading sins.

GENERAL MARKET

Before we look more carefully at types of general markets, let's talk a bit about what we mean by the *general market*. The truth is, there is nothing "general" about the stock market. It is a collective of very specialized market niches, each one of which has the capacity to sway the whole. Still, we are able to get a day-by-day picture of the market's consensus by looking at the various stock indexes. For the purposes of trend trading, we will need to look at only two primary indexes: the S&P 500 and the Nasdaq 100. To make things as simple as possible, I like to use charts of the exchange-traded fund (ETF) proxies for these indexes: SPY for the S&P 500 and QQQQ for the Nasdaq 100. You can also refer to the Dow Jones Industrial Average (whose ETF is DIA). It is a much-revered benchmark, and it does represent the country's 30 largest companies working the world's most productive industries. But it so closely shadows the S&P 500 that it needn't be a requisite part of our general market analysis.

More experienced traders can also add special market cap indexes and sector indexes to their analysis. If you want to do that, let me suggest that you also add the following charts to your general market watch list (again, put these in your Stockcharts.com or Clearstation.com watch lists for added convenience):

General Markets
- SPY (S&P 500)—tracks the 500 largest publicly traded companies

- QQQQ (Nasdaq 100)—tracks the 100 largest tech, biotech, and telecom companies

Market Cap Indexes
- MDY (S&P Midcaps)—tracks 400 representative midcap companies
- IWM (Russell 2000)—tracks 2,000 representative small-cap companies

Sector Indexes
- SMH—semiconductor companies
- IBB—biotech companies
- OIH—oil services companies
- HHH—Internet companies
- RTH—retail companies
- XLF—financial services companies
- XHB—home building companies

This is not an exhaustive list by any means, but it is a good start. These ETFs also make great trading vehicles, by the way. At Befriendthetrend.com, we offer The Index Newsletter, which trades these and other ETFs exclusively, including the brand-new *ultra* funds, which move in sync with the broader indexes but are leveraged at 2:1. I use several. Many subscribers use this letter to determine their sense of general market direction as well as profit from the trend-trade picks listed there. But if you would rather determine general market direction on your own, we give you here the rules for doing so.

Assume, for the sake of convenience, that you are

going to use SPY and QQQQ as your primary indicators of general market direction. Over the course of several years of watching and trading these broader indexes, we have come to note five different types of market conditions. They are:

- Bullish strongly trending
- Bullish weakly trending
- Bearish strongly trending
- Bearish weakly trending
- Range-bound (or nontrending)

In general, we want to focus on long plays in the first two types of market, short plays in the next two types, and a mix of longs and shorts in the last type of market. Let's first define the parameters of these different market types.

BULLISH: STRONGLY TRENDING

The Focus   It should be on long setups, particularly breakout plays (to be explained later).

Characteristics   This is everyone's favorite kind of market—except, of course, those "permabears" who always think the U.S. economy is going to collapse at any moment. This is the sort of market that sparked the day-trading frenzy in the late 1990s: everything goes up, and up a lot, nearly every day. The bulls are completely in control and win every battle with the bears. Making money is easy in a bullish strongly trending market, as long as you have the right entry system. But the drawback is that when this kind of market reaches a top, the sell-off can be quick and harsh and can wipe out months of hard-won gains in a matter of days. So in a strong bull market you must always be careful to play defensively against a possible reversal of momentum.

What to Look For Bullish strongly trending markets are easy to spot. Here are the key indicators:

- The 20 MA is above the 50 MA.
- Both the 20 MA and the 50 MA are rising.
- The distance between the 20 MA and the 50 MA is large and/or getting larger.
- Pullbacks in price reach only to the 20 MA, or at the most between the 20 MA and 50 MA; they do not reach all the way to the 50 MA.

How to Play It Use one of our systems as outlined later. Here we can say that a bullish strongly trending market is a great market to be in if you are already long. But if you are coming late to the party (and hopefully not too late), your best play is to look for stocks that are breaking out to new highs from periods of consolidation. You must make sure these breakout plays are confirmed by the various technical indicators we use. If price is making a new high but the indicators are not making new highs, then you have bearish divergence and you should move on to another chart.

Chart Example The chart of SPY in Figure 7.1 shows a classic bullish strongly trending market. Note that the 20

Figure 7.1 SPY—bullish: strongly trending.

MA (dotted line) is above the 50 MA (solid line), and that both MAs are in a rising uptrend. Further, the 20 MA is quite far away from the 50 MA, and the distance between is getting larger rather than smaller. Finally, note that the mid-August pullback and the two pullbacks in September traveled only as far as the 20 MA before the trend upward resumed again.

BULLISH: WEAKLY TRENDING

The Focus   It should be on long setups, particularly pull-back plays (to be explained later).

Characteristics   This is a tougher market to trade, since the pullbacks tend to be more frequent, steeper, and longer-lived. In a weakly trending market, corrections can last a couple of weeks. This can be frustrating if you are sitting on open long positions. Ultimately, the bulls are in control, but it can seem for days on end that the bears have moved in and made themselves right at home. However, this is one of the best markets in which to find great risk/reward scenarios in our setups. Those lengthier pullbacks serve to take a lot of the risk out of a trade, so our stop-loss can be closer to entry, and our exit targets can be that much further away.

What to Look For   Bullish weakly trending markets are not quite as obvious as their strong counterparts, but with some experience you should be able to recognize them. Here are the key indicators:

- The 20 MA is mostly (though not always) above the 50 MA.
- The 50 MA is rising, but the 20 MA is fluctuating (though mostly rising).
- The distance between the 20 MA and the 50 MA changes frequently.
- Pullbacks reach all the way to the 50 MA (sometimes beyond but only briefly).

How to Play It   Use one of our systems outlined later. Here we can say that a bullish weakly trending market is an ideal market for trend trading. You should find stocks that are showing strong trending action (normally stronger than the general market itself) but have pulled back to an area of support. This pullback should be confirmed by oversold indicators, and the current daily candlestick should put in a reversal bar of some kind before you consider an entry.

Figure 7.2   SPY—bullish: weakly trending.

Chart Example   The chart of SPY in Figure 7.2 shows a classic bullish weakly trending market. Note that the 20 MA remains above the 50 MA, and that the 50 MA is clearly in a rising uptrend. But also note that there are fluctuations in the 20 MA, indicating that sell-offs in the index are quite sharp and deep. You should also note that the various pullbacks seen in every month of this chart period traveled as far as the 50 MA, and sometimes beyond, before the trend upward resumed.

BEARISH: STRONGLY TRENDING

The Focus   It should be on short setups, particularly breakdown plays (to be explained later).

Characteristics   This is perhaps the most difficult market to trade. There are two reasons for this. First, bear markets always fight the long-term trend of the stock market (which is up) and, as such, tend to be short-lived. The second reason has to do with the extremely volatile nature of short-covering. Strong downtrends can cause a market to get so oversold so quickly that automated buy programs kick in to scoop up cheap shares. This causes traders and fund managers to cover their short positions in order to lock in profits. As they do so, they are forced to buy back shares they have borrowed, and the result is a sharp and quick short-covering rally (what traders call a *dead cat bounce*). But the advantage of bearish strongly trending markets is that they tend to go down faster than bullish strongly trending markets go up. When the bears are in control of a market, as they are in this type of market, they tend to go wild and overdo things. Can you blame them? For over 200 years, they have had to play second fiddle to the flashier bulls, and finally this is their chance in the spotlight. But you can take advantage of this. If you are willing to play the short side—to trend-trade for a living you *must* be willing to short—you can potentially make a lot more money in less time in a bearish strongly trending market than in any other type of market. And it is always a thrill to make money while 90 percent of the investing world is losing theirs.

What to Look For   A bearish strongly trending market is as easy to spot as its bullish cousin. Here are the key indicators:

- The 20 MA is below the 50 MA.
- Both the 20 MA and the 50 MA are falling.
- The distance between the 20 MA and the 50 MA is large and/or getting larger.

- Rallies reach only to the 20 MA or, at the most between the 20 MA and the 50 MA.

How to Play It   Use one of our systems outlined later. Here we can say that a bearish strongly trending market is a great market to be in if you are already short. But if you are coming late to the party (and hopefully not too late), your best play is to look for stocks that are breaking down to new lows from periods of consolidation. You must make sure these breakdown plays are confirmed by the various technical indicators we use. If price is making a new low, but the indicators are not making new lows, then you have bullish divergence and you should move on to another chart.

Chart Example   The chart of SPY in Figure 7.3 shows a classic bearish strongly trending market. Note that once the bear market begins in earnest in late April, the 20 MA

Figure 7.3   SPY—bearish: strongly trending.

Figure 7.4   SPY—a quick rally ends the bearish trend.

crosses below the 50 MA and remains there throughout the period. Also note that both MAs are falling, and that the 20 MA is falling at a faster pace than the 50 MA. You should also note that the various rallies seen in this chart, once the strong trend is established, travel only as far as the 20 MA before the dominant trend downward resumes.

As a follow-up, keep in mind our previous warning: bearish strongly trending markets can end very abruptly if a short-covering frenzy sets in. Check out what happened just two weeks after SPY tested the 20 MA in a bearish strongly trending market: instead of resuming the dominant trend, it reversed and killed it.

BEARISH: WEAKLY TRENDING

The Focus   It should be on short setups, particularly rallies into resistance (to be explained later).

Characteristics   This is an easier bear market to trade than the strongly trending version, since the rallies into resistance that trigger our setups take a lot of the risk out of the trade. But it still suffers from the two problems associated with bear markets we mentioned previously. In a weakly trending market, corrections (rallies) can last a couple of weeks, which can be frustrating if you are sitting on open short positions. Ultimately, the bears are in control, but it can seem for days on end that the bulls have moved in and made themselves right at home. However, just like its bullish cousin, this is one of the best markets in which to find great risk/reward setups. Those lengthier corrections to the dominant trend serve to take a lot of the risk out of a trade, so our stop-loss can be closer to entry, and our exit targets can be that much farther away.

What to Look For   Bearish weakly trending markets are also easy to spot. Here are the key indicators:

- The 20 MA is mostly (though not always) below the 50 MA.
- The 50 MA is falling, but the 20 MA is fluctuating (though mostly falling).
- The distance between the 20 MA and the 50 MA changes frequently.
- Rallies reach all the way to the 50 MA (sometimes beyond but only briefly).

How to Play It   Use one of our systems outlined later. Here we can say that a bearish weakly trending market is a good market for trend trading. You should find stocks that are showing strong downwardly trending action (normally stronger than the general market itself) but have rallied up into an area of resistance. This rally should be confirmed by overbought indicators. The daily candlestick should put in a reversal bar of some kind before you consider an entry.

Chart   The chart of SPY in Figure 7.5 shows a classic bearish weakly trending market. Note that the 20 MA remains for the most part below the 50 MA. There is a period in February where the 20 MA rises above the 50 MA—a sign that the index might be moving into a range-bound condition. But then the trend resumes with another bearish crossover. Note that the 50 MA is clearly in a falling trend throughout the period. Also note that there are fluc-

Figure 7.5   SPY—bearish: weakly trending.

tuations in the 20 MA, indicating that the rallies in the index are quite sharp and prolonged. These various rallies traveled as far as the 50 MA, and sometimes beyond, before the trend downward resumed again.

RANGE-BOUND (NONTRENDING)

The Focus   It should be on both long and short setups, particularly trendline breakout/breakdown plays (to be explained later).

Characteristics   Range-bound markets are the bane of a buy-and-holder's existence, but for the technical trader they are a godsend. This is because the technical indicators we use (stochastics, CCI, RSI) register overbought and oversold signals that work most robustly in range-bound markets. Moreover, if you are willing to trade more frequently, you can make a lot of money in a range-bound market. It is essential therefore to learn how to identify range-bound markets, because the general market spends a majority of its time in such a condition. In a range-bound market, price bounces up and down between roughly parallel pivot points of support (on the low side) and resistance (on the high side). Such a market suggests that bulls and bears are waging a war with each other, but no one side is clearly winning. Trading ranges between parallel pivot points can be either wide or narrow, and it is a general rule that the wider the trading range, the longer price stays within it. Narrower ranges tend to be broken to the upside or downside more easily.

What to Look For   Range-bound markets are not always easy to spot, but there are rules to follow. Here are the key indicators:

- The 20 MA spends about as much time above as below the 50 MA.
- The 50 MA is mostly flat, while the 20 MA varies from rising to falling.
- The distance between the 20 MA and the 50 MA varies greatly.
- Rallies and sell-offs easily pass through both moving averages.

How to Play It   Use one of our systems outlined later. Here it can be said that it is frustrating for traders when a range-bound market first appears, especially when it follows a strong up- or downtrend. Traders can be reluctant to transition from a fast-money, momentum environment (strong trend) to the more strategic, labor-intensive environment of the range-bound condition. But once the trading range is established, it can be an ideal trading environment. In a trading range, we use trendlines to highlight and delimit the minitrends within the range and our technical indicators to spot oversold and overbought levels as well as bullish and bearish divergence. We are looking to play reversals right off the pivot points of support and resistance, confirmed by a break of the intrarange trendline. Indicator divergence is often a key to locating the best reversal trades and will often let us pinpoint with extreme accuracy the tops and bottoms of movements within the range.

Chart   The chart of SPY in Figure 7.6 shows a rather wide trading range or range-bound condition. Note that the 50 MA remains relatively flat throughout this period, while the 20 MA bounces up and down following price. Also note that price does not pause much at either moving average but for the most part continues up and down as if they were not even there (in trending markets the MAs tend to act as support and resistance). That snake-ish look to the 20 MA, up and down like a roller coaster, is a telltale sign that we are in a range-bound market.

Once you understand the type of market you are currently trading in, you will have a better sense of the type of trade to look for: long or short, breakout or breakdown, pullback to support or rally into resistance, and so on. As indicated at the beginning of this section, this piece of your trading strategy is far from being the most important. The

Figure 7.6   SPY—trading range.

vital key to your success as a trend trader is finding the best-looking chart, regardless of what the rest of the market is doing. But if you can consistently get yourself on the same side as the market's net money flow, you will give your trading an extra edge. Sometimes that can make the difference between long-term success and a short-term wipeout.

PUT YOUR MARKET-
READING SKILLS TO
THE TEST

IN the following pages I am going to display a number of charts from the ETF proxies that represent the three primary stock averages: SPY (S&P 500), DIA (Dow Jones Industrial Average), and QQQQ (Nasdaq 100). Take a piece of paper and jot down what market type you think each chart displays. It might be helpful first to review the rules for each of the market types.

Bullish: Strongly Trending
- The 20 MA is above the 50 MA.
- Both the 20 MA and the 50 MA are rising.
- The distance between the 20 MA and the 50 MA is large and/or getting larger.
- Pullbacks reach only to the 20 MA or, at the most, between the 20 MA and 50 MA.

Bullish: Weakly Trending
- The 20 MA is mostly (though not always) above the 50 MA.
- The 50 MA is rising, but the 20 MA is fluctuating (though mostly rising).

- The distance between the 20 MA and the 50 MA changes frequently.
- Pullbacks reach all the way to the 50 MA (sometimes beyond but only briefly).

Bearish: Strongly Trending

- The 20 MA is below the 50 MA.
- Both the 20 MA and the 50 MA are falling.
- The distance between the 20 MA and the 50 MA is large and/or getting larger.
- Rallies reach only to the 20 MA or, at the most, between the 20 MA and 50 MA.

Bearish: Weakly Trending

- The 20 MA is mostly (though not always) below the 50 MA.
- The 50 MA is falling, but the 20 MA is fluctuating (though mostly falling).
- The distance between the 20 MA and the 50 MA changes frequently.
- Rallies reach all the way to the 50 MA (sometimes beyond but only briefly).

Range-Bound

- The 20 MA spends about as much time above as below the 50 MA.
- The 50 MA is mostly flat, while the 20 MA varies from rising to falling.
- The distance between the 20 MA and the 50 MA varies greatly.

- Rallies and sell-offs easily pass through both moving averages.

Now, see how many of the following charts (Figures 8.1–8.20) you can correctly identify. The correct answers are located after the charts, along with commentary. Note that some of these charts will show transitional periods between one type and another. To answer correctly in these cases you will need to identify both market types on either side of the transition. There may be a few charts that clearly show more than two types of market. So think carefully about your answers. Review the rules and stay focused!

1. Dow Jones Industrials, 2006

Figure 8.1   Trend Test Chart 1.

2. S&P 500, 1998

Figure 8.2   Trend Test Chart 2.

3. S&P 500, 2000

Figure 8.3   Trend Test Chart 3.

4. S&P 500, 2006

Figure 8.4   Trend Test Chart 4.

5. Dow Jones Industrials, 2005

Figure 8.5   Trend Test Chart 5.

6. Nasdaq 100, 2006

Figure 8.6   Trend Test 6.

7. Dow Jones Industrials, 2000

Figure 8.7   Trend Test Chart 7.

8. Dow Jones Industrials, 2004

Figure 8.8   Trend Test Chart 8.

9. Nasdaq 100, 2004

Figure 8.9   Trend Chart 9.

10. S&P 500, 2005

Figure 8.10   Trend Test Chart 10.

11. Nasdaq 100, 2001

Figure 8.11   Trend Test 11.

12. Dow Jones Industrials, 2006

Figure 8.12   Trend Test Chart 12.

13. Nasdaq 100, 2006

Figure 8.13   Trend Test Chart 13.

14. Dow Jones Industrials, 2004

Figure 8.14   Trend Test Chart 14.

15. Nasdaq 100, 2004

Figure 8.15   Trend Test Chart 15.

16. Nasdaq 100, 2001

Figure 8.16   Trend Test Chart 16.

17. Dow Jones Industrials, 1999

Figure 8.17   Trend Test Chart 17.

18. Dow Jones Industrials, 2003

Figure 8.18   Trend Test Chart 18.

19. Nasdaq 100, 2005

Figure 8.19   Trend Test Chart 19.

20. Nasdaq 100, 1999

Figure 8.20   Trend Test Chart 20.

Remember, these answers and their supportive commentary are the products of my own subjective readings of
the charts based on many years of active trading experience. As mentioned, chart reading is not an exact science.
Subjectivity is involved no matter how many rules are
applied. Nevertheless, a conscientious application of the
rules we laid out should keep us more or less on track. In
trading we are not looking for exactitude. Precision is not
an available commodity on the trading floor. All that is
needed to be hugely profitable in the trading game is to be
right more often than wrong.

Here are the answers as I see them (feel free to argue,
but you better have some good reasons for doing so!). Give
yourself points for every market type you get right:

1. This is clearly a *bullish strong trending* market, no questions asked. [1 point]

2. This one is a bit harder to decipher. The left side of the chart shows a straightfoward *bullish strong trend*. Then things get fuzzier. The market goes into a tight consolidation that could be called *range-bound*, but because there is not much snake-ish action from the 20 MA it is really more a period of transition. From there we have two possibilities. Either the market goes into a short-lived *bullish strong trend*, followed quickly by a *bearish strong trend*, or the market transitioned into the initial phase of a wide *range-bound* condition. More time is needed to confirm which possibility is correct. Give yourself credit if you gave either answer (in fact, the market went into a wide trading range in late 1998). [2 points]

3. Here we see a *range-bound* market. While the general trend is modestly upward, we see enough variation in the 50 MA to hesitate in calling it trending. The 50 MA is the key to the trending market: it should show no hesitation in moving up or down (a bit of flatness is okay, but it should never move countertrend). Certainly the 20 MA is "snakey" enough to allow us to get in some trendline breakout and breakdown plays. [1 point]

4. Clearly a *bullish strong trend*. What a beauty of a chart! [1 point]

5. Another *range-bound* market. Note the up and down twists of the 20 MA. [1 point]

6. Another clear *bullish strong trend*. It took a bit for this one to get started, but when price pulled back on September 11 to touch the 20 MA, then pushed off again, we got the confirmation that this was indeed a market with the bulls in control. [1 point]

7. Again, a *range-bound* market, as shown by the 50 MA, which just refuses to confirm an uptrend. Things did get strongly bullish in late September for a week or so, but once price pulled back and closed below the 50 MA, that possibility was negated. [1 point]

8. *Range-bound*, very clear. Look at that 20 MA: snake-city! [1 point]

9. There is a lot going on in this chart. Here we have five distinct market types: how many did you name? Clearly, on the left side of the chart we are in *range-bound* territory. That is easy enough. But then a sharp drop in the index in July and August tempts us to say we are in a *bearish strong trend*. This gets confirmed when price kisses the 20 MA on a relief rally and then plunges lower and the 50 MA shows a downward slope. So that's the second market type. But the trend gets negated pretty quickly once price shoots up above the 50 MA in early September. At this point we would have to say we are back to a *range-bound* market, only the range is now wider. But then the index keeps going up, and the first pullback in late September bounces cleanly off the 50 MA without going through it. This gives us our fourth market type: a *bullish weak trend*. We hold to this view until mid-October, when some

consolidation brings the index down to the 20 MA area. Here it holds before pushing strongly higher. The fact that it never went all the way to the 50 MA means that now, on the right side of the chart, we are in a *bullish strong trend*. This clearly gets confirmed as the index continues to climb higher, and the 20 MA moves further and further away from a rising 50 MA. Give yourself one point for each market type you recognized (in the right order). [5 points]

10. *Range-bound.* No questions asked. [1 point]

11. *Bearish strong trend.* No doubt about it. [1 point]

12. This chart is a bit more interesting. It starts with an obvious *bullish weak trend*. Note the frequent pullbacks to the 50 MA, which is in a consistent uptrend. But then the chart morphs into a *range-bound* condition as it consolidates all that upward movement and the 50 flattens out. By mid-July we might be tempted to call the early part of that transition a *bearish weak trend*, since the 50 MA area came close to holding as resistance and it is starting to roll over to the downside. But the fact that on its second relief rally later that month the index was easily able to pass through the 50 MA leads us to confirm that we are still within a trading range rather than starting a new trend. [2 points]

13. We see a *range-bound* initially, then the chart falls off quickly into a *bearish strong trend* as that tight range breaks to the downside. The trading range

seen here is very tight, and as such it is one of the worst kinds of market environments to trade in. Range-bound conditions are great for trend trading, as long as the range is wide enough to permit both longs and shorts sufficient time to bring our trailing stop-losses into profit territory. But the kind of tight range seen here is next to impossible to profit from unless you are a day trader. When we are in a tight range-bound market, we therefore need to find charts on our watch list that are not range-bound but which are showing sizeable moves either up or down. [2 points]

14. This chart starts with a *bullish weak trend* that then morphs into a *bullish strong trend*. Either way, it is a nice market for longs. [2 points]

15. A *bullish weak trend* is clearly seen here. [1 point]

16. Here we have a *bearish strong trend* that then reverses sharply and becomes a *bullish strong trend*. The fulcrum on which this strong reversal pivots is, of course, the terrorist attacks on the United States that took place on September 11, 2001. You can see clearly the gap down that took place after the markets reopened (they were closed for four days after the attacks) and subsequent selling pressure that led the index to make a deep cut low. From there, the index rallied over 50 percent in a few short weeks. We were able to position ourselves for this ramp-up, by the way—even before the strong

trend was confirmed—by looking at bullish divergence in the indicators. [2 points]

17. A *bullish strong trend*, which then consolidates in a *range-bound* condition. [2 points]

18. A *bullish strong trend* that then flattens out and morphs into a *bullish weak trend*. Note the transition that takes place between the two markets. In July we see some price consolidation after the sharp upward ramp. The 20 MA begins to flatten out, and the index moves all the way into the 50 MA, even slightly beyond. But once the 50 MA held as support and the index rallied, we knew we were still in an uptrend; only now it would not likely be as strong as it had been in prior weeks. Again, strong trends play off the 20 MA, weak trends off the 50 MA. [2 points]

19. A *bearish weak trend* is clearly seen here. Note that this trend got a big kick start with a gap down in January. Also note how the 50 MA acts as resistance all the way through. [1 point]

20. Easy enough: a *range-bound* market (due to the fact that price moves so easily through the 50 MA) that by mid-August, with the first successful hold of the 50 MA as support, becomes a *bullish weak trend*. [2 points]

So, how did you do? Give yourself a point for every market type you correctly recognized. There are 32 market types represented in these 20 charts. Write me if you want to argue otherwise, but for now I am sticking with the assessments listed here.

Here is how you should score yourself:

30: Excellent!
Write me, I may have a job for you.
25–30: Very good!
With a bit more experience, you should become a great chart reader.
20–25: Not bad, but . . .
I would suggest rereading this chapter and spending some time looking at more charts before moving on.
15–20: Having a bad day?
Try drinking a strong cup of coffee and taking the test again.
<15: Don't quit your day job!
Blame the author of this book for not being clear enough!

GET STARTED IN
TREND TRADING

SELECTING BULLISH STOCKS TO TREND-TRADE

IN this section, I am going to introduce you to my top 10 technical setups. These are the setups we at Befriend thetrend.com have found over the years to be the best possible setups for trend trading. Each of these setups is proprietary. This doesn't mean that we have a copyright to them, or that they use any secret "black box" formula that we will reveal to you only at our really, really expensive seminars. Rather, it simply means that they have been uniquely designed by me ("Dr. Stoxx") and the Befriend thetrend.com team through long periods of rigorous backtesting *and* real-money trading. These are the setups we use daily to find the trades we recommend to our various newsletter subscribers, and that we also trade with real money in our Befriend the Trend Fund. While they use common technical elements—so common that any popular charting system can accommodate them—there is nothing common about their performance.

A *setup* here refers to a combination of price pattern—the way price paints a certain picture on the chart—and technical indicators that, together, give us the right conditions for predicting with reasonable confidence the future direction of a stock's price. Now just because you have a great-looking setup on a chart does not in any way guarantee that price will move in our predicted direction. But the following setups have been selected because they have, in the past, contributed to a healthy percentage of highly profitable trades. They are thus *high-probability* setups.

For each of these setups we are going to tell you several things. We will indicate which market type, of the types we studied in Chapter 8, each setup is best suited for. This doesn't mean that there is only one market type you should play the setup in—it only means that the market type indicated will give your trade the best possible edge. We will also give you the rules you need to identify the setup on your watch list (see Chapter 6 on setting up a watch list), including the rules needed to confirm your entry into the trade. We will also show you how to use a stock-screening tool to search for these setups. You will have to resort to this tool whenever your watch list fails to produce any examples of that particular setup. We will tell you in very specific terms exactly how and when to enter the setup as you initiate a new stock position. For each setup we will give you two or three charts to examine that illustrate what each of the setups looks like in live trading.

For the sake of convenience we have put our five bullish setups in this chapter and our five bearish setups in Chapter 10. In Chapter 11, we will be treating the all-important topic of how to properly enter and exit your positions in order to maximize your profits and minimize your risks.

Before beginning, if you are not familiar with Japanese candlestick terms, please go to one of the several free Web-based tutorials on the subject. Three that I can recommend are supplied by these Web sites:

- www.altavest.com
- www.stockcharts.com
- www.incrediblecharts.com

Candlestick formations factor quite prominently in several of our systems, so be sure that before you continue you are familiar with their basic terminology. There are dozens of candlestick formations that you could study, but I focus only on the following high-percentage formations:

- Doji
- Hammer
- Piercing
- Morning/evening star
- Engulfing

Once you have had your candlestick tutorial, you are ready to begin looking for our top 10 setups. We have divided these into two general types: five bullish setups and five bearish setups. If you are looking for trades on the long side, with the expectation that price will rise for several days after entry, then you will be looking for one of our bullish setups. If you are looking for trades on the short side, with the expectation that price will fall for several days after entry, then you will be looking for one of our bearish setups.

In certain market conditions you will not find many

setups, and sometimes none at all. In other market conditions, you will find dozens of tradable setups. It is best
always to maintain the mindset that you will take whatever
the markets give you. Following are the top five bullish
setups.

THE PULLBACK

Market Type   This setup is best used in:

* Bullish: strongly trending markets
* Bullish: weakly trending markets

Characteristics   This is one of my all-time favorite
setups. Its origins lie in a seminar I took back in 1996
under the tutelage of a now discredited stock market guru.
If we can bracket out the fact that the man was convicted
by the SEC of making fraudulent claims on his Web site,
it is fair to say that he put on a very helpful seminar back
then, at a very reasonable price. The essential tools I
learned there form the basis for this bullish setup. Its focus
is on uptrending stocks that have experienced a period of
minor weakness. This weakness may just be a spate of
profit taking, or it may be in response to news or an earnings announcement. Regardless, our assumption is that the
weakness is temporary and thus a buying opportunity.
Normally after a period of minor weakness—as measured
here by the stochastics indicator reaching an oversold
level—the dominant uptrend will reassert itself as traders
who missed out on the prior move use the dip to get on
board.

Key Indicators   In the pullback setup, there are three key indicators:

- First, you should identify an uptrending stock (see definition) that has pulled back either into an upsloping 20 MA, between the 20 MA and the 50 MA, or all the way to the 50 MA. If this pullback point coincides with, or lies near, an upsloping trendline drawn under the lows of the uptrend, so much the better.

> **Definition:** An *uptrending stock* is a stock that is making higher lows (and preferably higher highs, but, strictly speaking, this is not necessary) over at least the past three months. A *weakly uptrending stock* is an uptrending stock whose 20 MA is mostly rising and mostly above a consistently rising 50 MA. A *strongly uptrending stock* is an uptrending stock whose 20 MA is always rising and always above a consistently rising 50 MA. The further these two moving averages are from each other, the stronger the uptrend.

- Second, along with the price pullback there must be a sharp dip in the stochastics indicator (5,3 period) to or below the oversold 20 line. This confirms that the stock is in an oversold condition.
- Third, the current candlestick must register a bullish reversal candle of some kind (hammer, engulfing, piercing, or doji). If the current

candlestick shows a bearish candle, or a red or black candle of any kind (close lower than the open), then this is a wait-and-see condition. You should make a note to check that stock again the next trading day.

- *Buy signal:* These three factors register a buy signal, and the stock is ready to be short-listed as a valid pullback play.

The Screening Tool   The pullback setup occurs most often in bullish weakly trending markets that have suffered a short period of price consolidation or profit taking. They can also occur in strongly uptrending markets in volatile stocks that tend to pull back further than the general market. There are occasions in the natural course of market cycles when pullback setups do not appear very often. If you fail to find any decent pullbacks on your primary watch list, you can try using a special screen to search the universe of stocks for them. To screen for pullback plays, input the following criteria into Stockcharts.com's screening tool:

- For the last market close:
- All stocks with . . .
  - 60-day simple moving average of volume for today is greater than 500,000.
  - 60-day simple moving average of close for today is greater than 15.
  - The chart has a bullish engulfing pattern for today (you can also run this with piercing, hammer, or doji selected as well).
  - 20-day simple moving average of close for today

is greater than 50-day simple moving average of
close for today.

- Daily close for today is less than daily close for
five days ago times 1.15.

This will normally give you a list of between two and
twenty stocks, depending on market conditions. If the list
is large, I will increase the 60-day moving average of volume to 1,000,000 and the daily close five days ago multiplier to 1.20. If the list is too small, I will decrease the
multiplier to 1.10 or less. It is not wise to go any lower than
500,000 on the moving average of volume.

If that scan fails to produce any viable pullback candidates, you can try this alternate scan:

- For the last market close:
- U.S. stocks with . . .
  - 20-day simple moving average of volume for to-
    day is greater than 1,000,000.
  - 60-day simple moving average of close for today
    is greater than 5.
  - 20-day simple moving average of close for today
    is greater than 50-day simple moving average of
    close for today.
  - 50-day simple moving average of close for today
    is greater than 200-day simple moving average
    of close for today.
  - 50-day simple moving average of close for today
    is greater than 50-day simple moving average of
    close for 10 days ago.
  - 200-day simple moving average of close for to-

day is greater than 200-day simple moving average of close for 20 days ago.

- Daily close for today is less than daily close for five days ago.
- Daily close for 7 days ago is greater than daily close for 20 days ago.
- Daily close for today is less than or equal to 20-day simple moving average of close for today.
- Daily close for today is greater than or equal to 50-day simple moving average of close for today.
- Daily open for today is less than or equal to daily close for today.
- Daily slow stoch %K (5, 3) for today is greater than daily slow stoch %D (5, 3) for today.

Figure 9.1   BRCM showing pullback setups.

Figure 9.1 is an example of a strongly uptrending stock, BRCM, which gave two pullback buy signals. Note that the stock is easily seen to be uptrending, and indeed is in a strong uptrend, with the rising 20 MA well above a rising 50 MA. We can see that on two occasions the stock pulled back to the 20 MA area and then put in a bullish candle: in the first signal there is a bullish engulfing candle, and in the second instance a doji. At both signals the stochastics dropped down to or below 20, signaling an oversold condition ripe for a reversal.

Figure 9.2 is another example of a strongly uptrending stock, QCOM, which gave one wait-and-see signal (first arrow) and two pullback buy signals. Note that the first of the two buy signals (second arrow) occurred in a

Figure 9.2   QCOM showing pullback setups.

strong uptrend but nevertheless got us in a bit prematurely, but a well-placed stop-loss (see Chapter 11) would have kept us in the trade. With a little patience, the trade eventually turned profitable. The second buy signal occurred during a weaker moment in the uptrend but still yielded a solid profit opportunity.

THE COILED SPRING

Market Type   This setup is best used in:

- Bullish: strongly trending markets
- Bullish: weakly trending markets
- Range-bound markets

Characteristics   This is sometimes known as a *bull flag* or *bull pennant* setup and sometimes as a *symmetrical triangle* pattern, depending on the shape of the coiled spring. For our purposes, we will lump all these together under a single setup. The premise of the coiled spring is that after a strong runup, a strong stock likes to take a breather as it consolidates the ramp-up in price. A weak stock will sell off, giving back much of its gains. But a strong stock likes to coil up in a sideways movement. As it does so, price tends to trend inside an ever tighter range—the spring coils up tighter and tighter—until shares are ready to climb again. When the coil finally springs open, it usually does so with a delightfully profitable burst of upward momentum.

Key Indicators   The pattern relies on a precise definition of what we mean by *coiled spring*. Here are the parameters:

- In the coiled spring setup, you are looking for a weakly uptrending to strongly uptrending stock (see previous setup for definition) that has recently put in a new high. By *recently* we mean within the past 20 trading days. This new high must be at least a new three-month high.
- Since setting that new high, the stock has consolidated inside a coiled spring (see definition). The coiled spring can be short and tight or drawn out and choppy, but the pattern requires the coil to be tightening up (the trading range is getting smaller) as it moves further to the right.

Definition: The *coiled spring* gets its name from the narrowing range the stock trades in over the last seven to twenty trading days as shares consolidate at or near its new high. This range can trade sideways or it can downtrend slightly, but it should not be trading at an upward angle. The key to the pattern is that the trading range, in general, is getting tighter and tighter.

- Note that in this setup we pay no attention to indicators. This is a pure pattern play. All we need are the two moving averages, the 20 MA and the 50 MA, and some trendlines.
  - Use the moving averages to determine that the stock is weakly or strongly uptrending (see preceding definition).
  - Draw in trendlines over the top and bottom of the coiled spring. It should form a triangular

shape of some kind due to the narrowing trading range of the coil but should not be angled
upward.

- It is essential that the coiled spring last at least
  seven but no more than 20 trading days. It is also
  essential that no part of the coil extend to or
  beyond the 50 MA. It can pass over the 20 MA,
  but not the 50 MA.
- *Buy signal:* The coiled spring itself puts the stock
  on the shortlist. A break of the trendline drawn
  over the tops of this coil marks the buy signal. A
  close below the lower trendline negates the coiled
  spring, and so we delete it from our watch list.

The Screening Tool   The coiled spring setup is not
often seen among high-beta or volatile stocks, so it will not
show up much on your primary watch list. But you can
screen for such stocks by inputting the following parameters into Stockcharts.com's screener:

- For the last market close:
- All stocks with . . .
  - 60-day simple moving average of volume for to-
    day is greater than 500,000.
  - 60-day simple moving average of close for today
    is greater than 10.
  - Daily close for today is greater than or equal to
    daily open for today.
  - Daily high for today is less than or equal to
    daily high for five days ago.

- Daily low for today is greater than or equal to daily low for five days ago.
- 20-day simple moving average of close for today is greater than 50-day simple moving average of close for today times 1.08.

Here is an alternate screen that also can turn up some nice coiled spring setups:

- For the last market close:
- All stocks with . . .
  - 60-day simple moving average of volume for today is greater than 500,000.
  - 60-day simple moving average of close for today is greater than 10.
  - 50-day simple moving average of close for today is less than 20-day simple moving average of close for today.
  - Daily Average Directional Index (ADX) line (14) for today is less than daily ADX line (14) for 20 days ago times 0.41.

In a market moving mostly sideways, you may return 10 to 15 stocks per day with these screens. But in most market conditions, your list will be a short one, and not all the stocks that turn up on this screen are really coiled springs. Give each chart that turns up on the screen a good eyeballing, and use the aforelisted rules to eliminate all but the most coiled of springs.

One thing to watch out for is that the trading range

within the coil is generally getting smaller (less intraday movement). The intraday lows should be getting a bit higher, and/or the highs a bit lower. You can have a wide range bar or two in this range, but that should be the exception, not the rule. Generally speaking, the longer the coiled spring is strung out, the higher it will rise after the spring has sprung. But coiled springs longer than 20 days in duration tend to indicate indecision on the part of investors and are best avoided.

Figure 9.3 is an example of a stock, ALVR, showing a coiled spring setup that triggered a successful buy signal once price broke above the trendline drawn over the tops of the coil. Note that the coil is a consolidation of a recent price high in an uptrend, is getting tighter, does not violate the 50 MA, and in this case is trending slightly downward. While this run to over 10.50 yielded a +16 percent return

Figure 9.3   ALVR showing coiled spring setup.

in less than two weeks, the stock continued higher and is currently trading +55 percent higher than the entry price.

FORD (Figure 9.4) shows another coiled spring example. Note that the 20 MA is rising and is nicely above a rising 50 MA, showing the stock to be in a strong uptrend. Also note that candlestick tails can poke out of the coil as long as the open and close of each candle stays within it. Again, a buy signal is triggered once price trades above the upper trendline. In this case the trade yielded over +50 percent in about one month.

Figure 9.5 is an example of another stock, CME, that shows two coiled springs. Note the sideways to slightly downtrending movement that marks the coiled spring, and how many of the candles are getting smaller relative to previous candles seen in the uptrend. Note also the buy signals as they print just above the resistance lines.

Figure 9.4   FORD showing coiled spring setup.

Figure 9.5   CME showing two coiled spring setups.

THE BULLISH DIVERGENCE

Market Type   This setup is best used in:

- Range-bound markets
- Bullish: weakly trending markets
- Bearish: weakly trending markets

Characteristics   This setup is really a workhorse for us. We can use it in all sorts of markets, even bearish ones. The markets spend most of their time in range-bound or weakly trending conditions, and this setup works in those conditions very well. As swing traders, we use the bullish divergence setup to pinpoint the bottoms of deep pullbacks (beyond the 50 MA) within long-range uptrends (see following definition). We will also use a version of it in another setup discussed later. Truly, the divergence tool is a very handy one indeed. The bullish divergence setup looks at a stock that is trading within a long-range uptrend, but which is currently in a substantial sell-off and has just put in a series of lower lows. This downtrending series needs to be at least two lows long so that there is a basis for comparison. Of course, too many lower lows will eventually negate the long-range uptrend, and thus nullify this setup.

Key Indicators   This setup relies on both price patterns and a variety of technical indicators. Here are the specifics:

- First, we need to identify the stock as being in a *long-range uptrend* (see definition). This supports the idea that the deep pullback we enter on is only a temporary aberration.

> **Definition:** The easiest way to identify a *long-range uptrend* is to note on the daily chart that the 50 MA (either rising or falling) is trading above a rising 200 MA. Note: It is key that the 200 MA is rising; this signals the uptrend. Once the 50 MA crosses under the 200 MA, even if the 200 MA is rising, the long-range uptrend is negated.

- Next, the bullish divergence setup is valid when price does three things:
  1. It trades below the 50 MA.
  2. It puts in at least two clear price lows during that pullback, with at least five trading days between the lows.

3. The last price low corresponds with a higher low in two or more of the following technical indicators: MACD, MACD histogram, stochastics, RSI, OBV, and CCI (at the settings we specified earlier).

• Note that if the last (lower) price low corresponds with the 200 MA, trendline support, or prior price support, so much the better.

• *Buy signal:* When the aforementioned conditions have been met, a buy signal is triggered when a bullish candle of some kind (doji, hammer, engulfing, morning star, etc.) is printed on the daily chart.

The Screening Tool   The following screen inputted into Stockcharts.com's stock screener will identify potential bullish divergence candidates:

• For the last market close:
• All stocks with . . .
    • 60-day simple moving average of volume for today is greater than 500,000.
    • 60-day simple moving average of close for today is greater than 10.
    • Daily low for yesterday is less than daily low for 20 days ago.
    • Daily low for yesterday is less than daily low for three days ago.
    • Daily MACD histogram (12,26,9) for today is greater than daily MACD histogram (12,26,9) for 15 days ago.

- Daily CCI (20) for today is greater than daily CCI (20) for 15 days ago.
- Daily RSI (5) for today is greater than daily RSI (5) for 15 days ago.
- 50-day simple moving average of close for today is greater than 200-day simple moving average of close for today.
- Daily open for today is less than daily close for today.

In Figure 9.6, FWLT registers a nice bullish divergence setup following a blow-off double bottom with a lower price low coupled with three cases of bullish divergence in the indicators: MACD, RSI, and CCI. Note that on the day of entry the 50 MA (dotted line), though falling, is still above a rising 200 MA (solid line), and that on the day prior to entry we have a bullish candlestick marking the second low (hammer candle). The shares went on to gain +25 percent in only 20 trading days.

In Figure 9.7, see BRCM, which gave two nice bullish divergence buy signals in the course of this choppy runup. The trigger candle for the first setup was a doji and for the second a hammer. Note that you need divergence on only two indicators to validate the play. It is also interesting to note that the buy-and-holder with shares held from the left side to the right side of this chart would have seen her position increase by +24 percent, a nice run. But consider what you would have gotten on two trend trades: +40 percent with a lot less time exposed to the risks of the market.

Figure 9.6 FWLT showing a bullish divergence setup.

Figure 9.7   BRCM showing bullish divergence setups.

THE BLUE SKY BREAKOUT

Market Type   This setup is best used in:

- Bullish: strongly trending markets

Characteristics   Also called a *cup-and-handle* formation,
this setup is sometimes your only play during prolonged
bull markets when there just doesn't seem to be any pullback. Some swing traders are forced by a strong bull market to sit on the sidelines day after day, waiting for a pullback
or price consolidation to give them setups. How frustrating
is that when all those buy-and-holders are gloating over
their gains! But trend traders have a key weapon in their
arsenal during such times: the blue sky breakout setup. *Blue
sky* here refers to the new high territory the stock trades up
into as it clears at least three months of prior price highs.
We confirm the breakout by looking at an indicator that
gives us a visual reference of recent trends in volume.

Key Indicators   This setup relies on five price parameters combined with one technical indicator: on balance volume (OBV). Here are the rules:

- First, the closing price of the stock (not just the
  intraday move) must register a new high
  following a previous new *pivot* high set *within*
  the past 20 trading days. A pivot high is a new
  price high followed by a sell-off or sideways
  consolidation of at least five bars (but not more
  than 20) in length. We set these limits because it
  is important that the new high be the result of a

recent and short-lived move in price rather than a
prolonged runup.

- Second, the current new closing price high must
  be a significant high; no higher closing price high
  should be recorded in at least the past three
  months of trading.
- Third, the new closing price high cannot have
  run too far above the 52-week low for the stock.
  We don't want stocks that are too overextended.
  To prevent this, we calculate a multiple by taking
  the new high closing price and dividing it by the
  52-week low price. This multiple should not be
  more than 3.0. In other words, if a stock's 52-
  week low is 10.00, we want to buy a blue sky
  breakout only if the new closing high is less than
  30.00.
- Fourth, the current breakout into blue sky
  territory (no price resistance within the previous
  three months) should be accompanied by the
  highest OBV reading seen in at least the past
  three months (see definition).

Definition: OBV stands for *on balance volume*.
It measures the accumulation or distribution of
shares: share volume is either added to (on up
days) or subtracted from (on down days) a running balance of volume. OBV confirms price
moves when it runs with price, and shows divergence when it runs against price. It tends to be a
leading rather than a lagging indicator and as
such is useful in predicting future price moves.

- Fifth, the candle on the day of the breakout to a new high must be a green or white candle (close higher than the open).
- *Buy signal:* When all five of these parameters have been met on the same day, we have a buy signal.

The Screening Tool   In a bull market, the following scan should turn up several possible blue sky candidates—but since that first price parameter cannot be screened for, a further eyeballing of the charts is usually required to weed out invalid setups:

- For the last market close:
- U.S. stocks with . . .
  - New 52-week high.
  - 20-day simple moving average of volume for today is greater than 500,000.
  - 60-day simple moving average of close for today is greater than 10.
  - Daily close for today is less than or equal to minimum low over 260 days starting today times 3.
  - Daily OBV for today is greater than daily OBV for 60 days ago.

In Figure 9.8, AAPL shows three blue sky breakout signals. This kind of stair-stepping or repetitive cup-and-handle pattern is common in strong, healthy uptrends and often precedes a lengthy and extended bullish run. Note that the new price highs were set within 20 days of a previous new high with at least three down days in between.

Figure 9.8   AAPL showing blue sky breakout setups.

Also note the new high seen in OBV in each case. Further note that by *new high* we mean on a closing basis rather than an intraday basis. Thus when drawing your lines on the price chart, put them over the tops of the closing prices rather than the upper "tails" of the candles. So healthy was this trend, in fact, that AAPL made it all the way to 86.40 before succumbing to profit taking.

Our second example, CREE, (Figure 9.9) shows a very profitable blue sky breakout. In late April, CREE set a new five-month pivot high at the 20.00 price level. After 16 days of consolidation, the bulls stepped up again to drive price higher. On April 22 we got our price breakout coupled with a new high in OBV. We actually called this one

Figure 9.9   CREE showing a blue sky breakout setup.

in our Trend Trade Newsletter, netting subscribers a quick +22 percent gain in 12 days. A longer hold could have banked something closer to +50 percent.

The blue sky breakout is truly a befriend-the-trend kind of setup, and certainly one of the most exciting setups to trade. But many traders are afraid to play this kind of breakout because they worry the shares are too overbought and extended. They needn't be. In a strongly uptrending market, your best bet is to "buy high and sell higher". Trends once begun tend to keep trending: this is the essence of trend trading. But to keep the odds in your favor, stick closely to the five rules we outlined above.

THE BULLISH BASE BREAKOUT

Market Type   This setup is best used in:

- Bullish: weakly trending markets
- Bearish: strongly trending markets
- Bearish: weakly trending markets
- Range-bound markets

Characteristics   This is another very useful setup that can be traded in a variety of markets. It nicely rounds out our series of bullish setups since it is not strictly a befriend-the-trend kind of setup. Rather, in this setup we are going to be contrarian, bucking the trend. Here we are looking for a stock that is in a downtrend but has put in an extended sideways base of some kind. The fact that the stock is now moving sideways instead of down makes this base a bullish one. To render the setup valid, we need the indicators to tell us two things about price behavior within the base: it has to be gaining in momentum, and there must be evidence that shares are under accumulation. While longer holds of this setup can return spectacular gains, there is often a quick burst of buying activity at the point of breakout that can bring gains of +10 percent or more within a few days, making this an ideal short-term, trend trade setup. Moreover, this setup is most often seen in lower-priced stocks, so it is an ideal setup for smaller account traders.

Key Indicators   This setup relies on a price pattern (bullish base) combined with two technical indicators: MACD and on balance volume (OBV). Here are the specifics:

- First, the stock must be clearly seen to be in a downtrend of some kind, strong or weak (see definition).

Definition: A *downtrending stock* is a stock that is making lower highs (and preferably lower lows, but, strictly speaking, this is not necessary) over at least the past three months. A *strongly downtrending stock* is a downtrending stock whose 20 MA is consistently falling and below a consistently falling 50 MA. A *weakly downtrending* stock is a downtrending stock whose 20 MA may be rising and falling, but it is at least mostly below a consistently falling 50 MA.

- Second, for at least the past 30 trading days (six weeks), price must be moving within a consolidation base of some kind. There are two types of consolidation bases: triangles and rectangles. These bases can occur in uptrends as well as downtrends. In this setup, we want to see these at the bottom of a downtrend.
  - Figures 9.10 and 9.11 are two types of rectan-

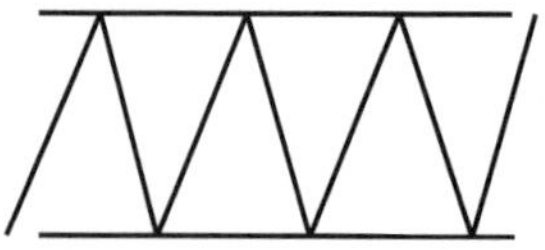

Figure 9.10   Flat rectangle base.

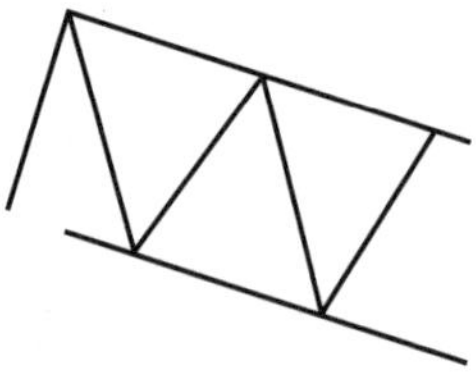

Figure 9.11   Falling rectangle base.

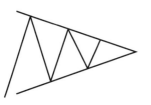

Figure 9.12 Symmetrical triangle base.

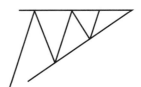

Figure 9.13 Ascending triangle base.

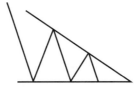

Figure 9.14 Descending triangle base.

gle bases seen in downtrending markets (flat and falling).

- Figures 9.12 through 9.14 are three types of triangle bases seen in downtrending markets (symmetrical, ascending, and descending.)
- The one type of consolidation pattern we want to avoid is the *rising wedge*, a type of triangle consolidation that occurs in downtrending stocks, but which usually precedes a continuation of the downtrend. A rising wedge does not form a valid base for this setup. Rising wedges look like Figure 9.15, where both trendlines slope upward.

Figure 9.15 Rising wedge: invalid base.

- Once we have identified a consolidation base in a downtrending stock, we need to confirm that it is a bullish base. We do this by referring to two technical indicators: MACD and OBV.
  - MACD must be making a series of higher lows while price is within the base may or may not be making higher lows.
  - OBV must rise above a trendline placed over the tops of the indicator.
- *Buy signal:* A buy signal is triggered in a bullish base at the first green or white candle (close higher than the open) after the candlestick on which the OBV trendline broke to the upside. You can also enter on the day of an OBV break if that candle is green or white.

The Screening Tool   It is not possible to screen for triangular or rectangular bases using what is commonly available. Most of your trades in this setup will have to come from your watch lists as you eyeball the charts. But the following screen will turn up a few decent candidates among many false hits that can be short-listed for further research. Readers who are more adept at this sort of thing than I am might want to fiddle around with these parameters to make them more robust.

- For the last market close:
- U.S. stocks with . . .
  - 20-day simple moving average of volume for today is greater than 500,000.

- 60-day simple moving average of close for today is greater than 10.
- 50-day simple moving average of close for today is greater than 20-day simple moving average of close for today.
- 50-day simple moving average of close for today is less than 50-day simple moving average of close for 40 days ago.
- Maximum range over 30 days starting today is greater than maximum range over 15 days starting today.
- Maximum range over 15 days starting today is greater than maximum range over 5 days starting today.
- Daily OBV for today is greater than daily OBV for 40 days ago.
- Daily MACD line (12,26,9) for today is greater than daily MACD line (12,26,9) for 40 days ago.
- 50-day simple moving average of close for today is less than 200-day simple moving average of close for today.

In the absence of a reliable screen, you will have to check the charts on your watch list on a regular basis. In fact, this is a better way to go because it allows you to watch a base develop over several days and weeks. That OBV trigger signal is really the key to this setup: if you can get in on the day that happens, you often will be in at the start of a significant rally. But the stocks that show up on the preceding screen most often have already triggered their OBV signal.

In Figure 9.16, AKS shows a weak downtrend coiling up within a bullish triangular (symmetrical) base. We can see that MACD shows higher lows (bullish confirmation) and that OBV triggered a buy signal after price broke up out of the base. From there the stock quickly climbed nearly 20 percent over seven trading days.

Figure 9.16   AKS showing a bullish base breakout setup.

In Figure 9.17, KLAC consolidates a strong downtrend capped by a nasty gap down within a bullish rectangular base. We know it is bullish because MACD, which measures price momentum, is rising throughout the base. OBV then gives a buy signal just prior to the base breakout. An entry around 42.00 would have returned a healthy +19 percent with the trade still open on a trailing stop. Note here how the upper trendline of bullish base (at a

Figure 9.17   KLAC shows a bullish base breakout setup.

Figure 9.18 JNPR showing a bullish base breakout setup.

price of 42.00), which acted as resistance while price remained within the base, now acts as support for the new uptrend.

Figure 9.18 shows a bullish base beakout setup that we offered subscribers to our Cheap Stocks Newsletter. JNPR's shares nicely formed a falling rectangular base within a clear downtrend (weak, becoming strong). The base shows bullish divergence in the MACD indicator, confirming that the base is a bullish one. When OBV triggered a breakout of its trendline, we had confirmation that shares of JNPR were being accumulated. Price often follows an OBV breakout, and, sure enough, shares of JNPR did just that. Shortly after the falling rectangle gave way, JNPR shares rocketed quickly upward for a return of nearly +30 percent in just six weeks.

SELECTING BEARISH STOCKS TO TREND-TRADE

SHORT SELLING

Short selling, or *shorting*, is an essential skill for trend traders. Technically, it is not much different from buying shares of a stock to open a position and then selling those shares back to the market to close the position. Only in short selling, you reverse that order: first you sell shares to the market, then to close the position you buy them back. If your open position trades down below your entry price, money will be credited to your account on the purchase of stock. If your open position trades up above your entry price, money will be taken out of your account to cover the loss.

Since you can only sell shares to the market that you already own, you must first borrow from your broker the shares needed to open a short position. Thus, whether your broker has the shares to borrow in the first place is an essential part of the short-selling equation: if your broker has no shares to lend, you have no shares to borrow in order to sell short. Generally, most good online brokers keep a healthy supply of shares to lend on all major, liquid stocks. The stocks we normally trade at Befriendthetrend.com are almost always available to short. Occasionally, however, you will find yourself in the frustrating predicament of having done a lot of research on a chart only to discover that you cannot open the position because your broker doesn't have shares to borrow. Even more frustrating is seeing that stock tank hard for days on end—without you on board. An alternative to selling the stock short, then, is buying put options on the stock. As explained in Part Four, buying puts on a stock is a way to profit from a selloff in the stock; and it is sometimes your only alternative when your broker is out of shares to borrow.

Some say that short selling is un-American or that it somehow hurts the general economy. Others say that it is beneficial to the overall health of the market in that it supplies much-needed liquidity to the buyers of stock, especially during prolonged bull markets. But I don't think you can make a strong case either way. For every buyer there must be a seller, and it makes little difference whether you sell your own shares or your broker's shares. In fact, when you sell your own shares, that terminates your relationship with the company and its public offerings. When you short using borrowed shares, you have, in fact, entered into a promissory agreement with that company to make a purchase of its shares at some point in the future (on behalf of your broker, of course, not your own account).

There is also the perception that short selling is a higher-risk activity than simply buying stock. The rationale behind this is that, while your long positions can go to zero and wipe out your entire investment, a short position can rally to infinity (in theory), thus wiping out not only your investment but all your cash reserves as well, not to mention every other asset you own. And then there is the numbers game: a stock that goes from $50 to $25 takes a 50 percent haircut off your investment; however, if that same stock sold short were to rally from $25 to $50, you are out 100 percent of your original investment.

Several things need to be said here in defense of short selling. First, there are easy ways of managing your short positions in order to play them defensively, which we will discuss later. These keep your losses to a minimum when a trade goes against you. Second, long before your entire account is wiped out, your broker is going to give you a *margin call* in the event that your short positions get to the point that they jeopardize your ability to trade (it is in your broker's best interests to keep you trading). In most margin calls, your broker will simply exit your positions for you if you don't do it yourself within a given time period. Third, far more companies go bankrupt and trade to penny stock status than soar to infinity, so the overall trend is on the side of relative safety. Fourth, the short-selling systems described here have at least a 70 percent success rate. They are oriented toward making money, not losing it. In short (pardon the pun), with the right trading and position management systems in place, the risks of short selling are far outweighed by the rewards.

TOP FIVE BEARISH SETUPS

If you are looking for trend trades on the short side, with the expectation that price will fall after entry, then you will be looking for one or more of the following setups. When you come across a stock on your watch list fitting one or more of these setups, jot it down on a piece of paper. Once you have finished eyeballing your primary watch list, you should have a short set of stocks you will then do further research on. You may also add to this list stocks that turn up on your special screens.

The Relief Rally

Market Type   This setup is best used in:

- Bearish: strongly trending markets
- Bearish: weakly trending markets

Characteristics   This setup is really the inverse of the pullback setup mentioned previously. Here we are looking for a stock that is strongly or weakly downtrending but has rallied up off its lows to reach a major moving average, which should act as resistance. We always wait to enter until we get confirmation of an overbought condition—as seen in the stochastics indicator—and a confirming bearish candlestick of some kind. The relief rally itself may just be a spate of short-term profit taking or a short squeeze (where shorts are forced to cover their positions and buy back shares due to a surprising reversal), or it may be in response to news or an earnings announcement. Regardless, once the reevaluation of shares plays itself out, the dominant trend usually emerges again. The odds of this happening are heightened when this play is put on when a bearish trend is seen in the broader market.

Key Indicators   In this setup there are three key ingredients:

- First, identify a strongly or weakly downtrending stock that has rallied up into a downsloping 20 MA (strongly downtrending) or 50 MA (weakly downtrending). If this moving average coincides with, or is placed near, a downsloping trendline placed over the highs of the downtrend, so much the better.

Definition: A *downtrending stock* is defined as a stock that is consistently making lower highs (and preferably lower lows, but, strictly speaking, this is not necessary). A *strongly downtrending stock* is a downtrending stock whose 20 MA is always falling and below a falling 50 MA. The further these two MAs are separated, the stronger the downtrend. A *weakly downtrending stock* is a downtrending stock whose 20 MA is mostly falling and is below a falling 50 MA.

- Second, there must be a sharp rise in stochastics (five-period) to or above the overbought 80 line.
- Third, the price on the rally to that moving average must have put in a bearish candle of some kind (doji, engulfing, gravestone, hanging man, evening star, etc.). If it has put in a green or white candle (close above the open), then this is a wait-and-see condition. You should make a note to check that stock again the next trading day.
- *Sell short signal:* These three factors register a sell short signal and the stock is ready to be short-listed as a valid relief rally setup.

The Screening Tool   There are occasions in the natural course of market cycles when relief rally setups do not appear very often. If you fail to find any decent relief rallies on your primary watch list, you can try using a special screen to search the universe of stocks for them. When I do this, I input the following criteria into Stockcharts.com's screening tool:

- For the last market close:
- All stocks with . . .
  - 60-day simple moving average of volume for today is greater than 500,000.
  - 60-day simple moving average of close for today is greater than 10.
  - The chart has a bearish engulfing pattern for today.
  - 20-day simple moving average of close for today is less than 50-day simple moving average of close for today.
  - Daily close for today is greater than daily close for five days ago times 1.15.

Normally, half a dozen stocks appear from this screen, depending on market conditions. If the list is too large, I will increase the volume to 1,000,000 and the daily close five days ago multiplier to 1.20. If the list is too small, I will decrease the multiplier to 1.10 or less.

Figure 10.1 is an example of a downtrending stock, NVDA, that gave two relief rally sell short signals: the first during a weak downtrend with a rally into the 50 MA, and the second after the trend got stronger with a relief rally only into the 20 MA. Also note that we have two bearish candle

Figure 10.1   NVDA showing two relief rally setups.

formations in both cases: a bearish engulfing at the first signal and a shooting star doji at the second signal. You will also
note that on July 9 there was an additional signal that failed
to yield the desired result, unless you used a wide stop-loss.

Figure 10.2 shows another example of a weakly becoming strongly downtrending stock, QLGC, which gave four
relief rally sell short signals within four months. It is rare to
get so many short signals in such a short time period, but
when they happen like this, it is a trader's dream come true.
Note that tightly trailing stops would have done well to lock
in substantial profits on at least three of the trades. A reasonable return on this sequence of trades is in the +50 to
+60 percent range, while the buy-and-holder had to sit
through a very uncomfortable 55 percent drawdown.

Figure 10.2 QLGC showing four relief rally setups.

The Bearish Divergence

Market Type   This setup is best used in:

- Range-bound markets
- Bearish: weakly trending markets
- Bullish: weakly trending markets

Characteristics   This setup is the flip side of its bullish cousin noted previously, and as such is also a great workhorse for us. We can use it in all sorts of markets, both bearish and bullish. As trend traders, we use the bearish divergence setup to pinpoint the tops of sharp rallies (beyond the 50 MA) within long-range downtrends. We will also use a version of it in another setup discussed later.

Truly, the divergence tool is a very handy one indeed. The bearish divergence setup looks at a stock that is trading within a long-range downtrend, but which is currently in a substantial rally, and has just put in a series of higher highs. This uptrending series needs to be at least two highs long so that there is a basis for comparison. Of course, too many higher highs will eventually negate the long-range downtrend and thus nullify this setup.

Key Indicators   This setup relies on both a price pattern and a variety of technical indicators. Here are the specifics:

- First, we need to identify the stock as being in a *long-range downtrend* (see definition). This supports the idea that the sharp rally we enter on is only a temporary aberration.

> **Definition:** The easiest way to identify a *long-range downtrend* is to note on the daily chart that the 50 MA, either rising or falling, is trading below a falling 200 MA. Note: It is essential that the 200 MA is falling; this signals the downtrend.

- Next, the bearish divergence setup is valid when price does three things:
  - It trades above the 50 MA.
  - It puts in at least two clear price highs during that rally, with at least five trading days between the highs.
  - The last price high corresponds with a lower high in two or more of the following technical

indicators: MACD, MACD histogram, stochastics, OBV, CCI, or RSI.
- Note that if the last (higher) price high
corresponds with the 200 MA, trendline
resistance, or prior price resistance, so much
the better.
- *Sell Short Signal:* When the preceding conditions
have been met, a sell short signal is triggered
when a bearish candle of some kind (doji,
gravestone, engulfing, evening star, etc.) is
printed on the daily chart.

The Screening Tool   When eyeballing your watch list
fails to turn up any relief rally setups, the following screen
inputted into Stockcharts.com's stock screener should identify several possible candidates:

- For the last market close:
- All stocks with . . .
  - 60-day simple moving average of volume for to-
    day is greater than 500,000.
  - 60-day simple moving average of close for today
    is greater than 10.
  - Daily high for yesterday is greater than daily
    high for 20 days ago.
  - Daily high for yesterday is greater than daily
    high for three days ago.
  - Daily MACD histogram (12,26,9) for today is
    less than daily MACD histogram (12,26,9) for
    15 days ago.
  - Daily ROC (12) for today is less than daily
    ROC (12) for 15 days ago.

- Daily RSI (14) for today is less than daily RSI (14) for 15 days ago.
- 50-day simple moving average of close for today is less than 200-day simple moving average of close for today.
- Daily open for today is greater than daily close for today.

In Figure 10.3, KLAC registers a bearish divergence setup for a successful swing trade. Note that the 50 MA is significantly below the 200 MA, signaling a strong

Figure 10.3   KLAC showing a bearish divergence setup.

downtrend, and that bearish divergence is seen between the two price highs and two key indicators (RSI and MACD histogram). Also note the bearish candle formation (evening doji reversal), which confirmed the sell short signal.

In Figure 10.4, Agilent (A) registers a bearish divergence setup for a successful swing trade, with bearish divergence seen between the two price highs (higher) and both the RSI and CCI indicators (lower). Note that this setup had the added attraction of price running up into a

Figure 10.4   A showing a bearish divergence setup.

downsloping 200 MA along with an area of former price resistance (20.00 area).

The Gap Down

Market Type   This setup is best used in:

- Bullish strong trending markets
- Bullish weakly trending markets
- Range-bound markets

Characteristics   The gap down setup employs a contrarian trading style. This setup trades stocks that are in strong uptrends but have just printed an *unfilled gap down*; that is, they gap down sharply at the open and fail during the day to close the gap. This setup requires that the gap down occur only after a significant new high (highest price for at least three months) has been established. This is the reason they work best in bull markets. Any stock climbing to new highs in a bear market is a safe-haven stock and should be avoided by short sellers. Frequently this setup signals a strong reversal of trend, as investors panic and rush to the exits in order to lock in profits in the wake of bad news, disappointing earnings, profit taking, and so on. This setup has a tendency to take a few days to get started as bears fend off the dip-buying crowd. But once they win control, and they usually do after a gap down, the drop can be sharp and fast.

Key Indicators   This setup is very easy to spot and trade. Here are the specifics:

- First, we need to identify the stock as being in a *steady uptrend*. For the purposes of this setup, we define a steady uptrend as follows:
  - The 50 MA is rising steadily without any major dips.
  - Price has remained above the 50 MA for at least the past 40 trading days (two months).
- Second, there needs to be an *unfilled gap down* on the current candlestick (see definition).

Definition: An *unfilled gap down* is identified when, on the market's close, a stock's intraday high price remains below the intraday low of the preceding day's trading.

- *Sell short signal:* When these conditions have been met, a sell short signal is triggered anytime after the gap down day when price trades below the intraday low of the gap down candlestick. Note: If at any time price trades up into the gap prior to triggering the sell signal, the setup is negated.

The Screening Tool   Several premium charting packages, including eSignal and Quote.com, offer an unfilled gap hotlist function, but this does not screen for uptrending stocks. However, the following screen parameters, when inputted into Stockcharts.com's stock screener, will search daily for gap down setups in uptrending stocks.

- For the last market close:
- All stocks with . . .

- Breakaway gap down.
- 60-day simple moving average of volume for to-day is greater than 500,000.
- 60-day simple moving average of close for today is greater than 10.
- 20-day simple moving average of close for today is greater than 50-day simple moving average of close for today times 1.1.

The chart of EBAY in Figure 10.5 shows the gap down setup following a strong uptrend. Note that the intraday high on the gap down day remained below the low of the previous trading day, and that the 50 MA is in a steady uptrend.

In Figure 10.6, we see what happened to EBAY shortly after the gap down setup was confirmed. Note that the day after the gap down setup was confirmed, EBAY

Figure 10.5   EBAY showing a gap down setup.

Figure 10.6   EBAY triggers a sell signal in a gap down setup.

Figure 10.7   SWIR showing a gap down setup.

gapped down again. With an opening price below the previous day's low, we had our entry signal. While it took a few days to consolidate the new bearish posture, once price resumed its new trend, it really took off.

The chart of SWIR in Figure 10.7 shows another gap down setup following a strong uptrend. Note that the gap down candlestick here is quite long, which may lead some to conclude that the position has already gone too far to warrant an entry. Never underestimate the power of a gap down. It is truly a trend killer. All that is needed to complete this setup is a trade below the low of the unfilled gap down day's candle.

Although it took three days to get moving again after that big red stick, and indeed to trigger our sell short entry signal, SWIR shows just how powerful the gap down setup can be (Figure 10.8). Note that SWIR's gap down into a

Figure 10.8   SWIR triggers a sell signal in a gap down setup.

rising moving average may have looked tempting to the "buy the dip" crowd. Consider this a warning: *never* buy a dip to support in an uptrending stock that takes place after an unfilled gap down, however strong the uptrend! You are likely to get caught in a bull trap.

The Blue Sea Breakdown

Market Type   This setup is best used in:

- Bearish: strongly trending markets

Characteristics   Think of this as a reverse cup-and-handle formation. Like its bullish cousin outlined in the previous chapter, this setup is sometimes your only play during prolonged bear markets when there just doesn't seem to be any relief in sight. *Blue sea* here refers to the new low territory the stock trades down into as it clears at least three months of prior price lows. We confirm the break-down by looking at an indicator that gives us a visual reference of recent trends in volume.

Key Indicators   This setup relies on five price parameters combined with one technical indicator: on balance volume (OBV). Here are the rules:

- First, the closing price of the stock (not just the intraday move) must register a new low following a previous new low set *within* the past 20 trading days. It is important that the new low be the result of a recent and short-lived move in price rather than a prolonged sell-off.

- Second, the current new closing price low must be a significant low; no low closing price low should be recorded in at least the past three months of trading.

- Third, the new closing price low cannot have run too far below the 52-week high for the stock. We don't want stocks that are too overextended to the downside. To prevent this, we calculate a multiple by taking the 52-week high and divide it by the new low closing price. This multiple should not be more than 2.0. In other words, if a stock's 52-week high is 30.00, we would sell short a blue sea breakdown only if the new closing low is greater than 15.00.

- Fourth, the current breakdown into blue sea territory (no price support within the previous three months) should be accompanied by the lowest OBV reading seen in at least the past three months.

- Fifth, the candle on the day of the breakdown to a new low must be a red or black candle (close is lower than the open).

- *Sell short signal:* When all five of the these parameters have been met on the same day, we have a sell short signal.

The Screening Tool   In bull markets this screen will not return many candidates, but in a strong bear market it should turn up several possible blue sea candidates. Since that first price parameter cannot be screened for, a further eyeballing of the charts is usually required to weed out invalid setups.

- For the last market close:
- U.S. stocks with . . .
  - New 52-week low.
  - 20-day simple moving average of volume for today is greater than 500,000.
  - 60-day simple moving average of close for today is greater than 5.
  - Daily close for today is greater than or equal to maximum high over 260 days starting today times 0.5.
  - Daily OBV for today is less than daily OBV for 60 days ago.

In Figure 10.9, JNPR shows a blue sea breakdown signal as it passes below a three-month low with confirming new low in the OBV indicator. An entry at the open of the next trading day could have been covered nine days later, for a maximum gain of +17 percent. The stock rallied shortly after that, so you would likely have been stopped out for something more like +12 percent.

In Figure 10.10, we see XMSR confirming a blue sea breakdown with supportive OBV on the last day of April. In this case, OBV first broke down to a new three-month low, and the stock price did not confirm the breakdown until the next day. However, once it confirmed—BAM!— the stock got a −50 percent haircut. Note that the stock is

JNPR (Juniper Networks) Nasdaq GS   © StockCharts.com
25-May-2006 4:00pm   **Last** 15.29 **Volume** 16.3M **Chg** +0.74 (+5.09%)▲

New 3-month price low + black candle + new 3 month OBV low = blue sea breakdownsetup

Figure 10.9   JNPR shows a blue sea breakout setup.

clearly in a steady downtrend as signaled by the steadily downsloping 50 MA. Neither moving averages nor trend-lines factor into this setup since a new three-month price low is evidence enough that we are in a downtrend.

One further thing to note about the XMSR chart in Figure 10.10 is just how abruptly the downtrend can end in a blue sea breakdown. With no immediate support under price, these trades tend to move down quickly and sharply. But when bottom-feeding hedgies (hedge fund traders) smell blood in the water, they like to move in with size, creating panic among the shorts. That is the power of short-covering: it is price manipulation at its worst and can wipe out weeks of gains on the short side in a matter of hours.

Figure 10.10   XMSR shows a blue sea breakout setup.

If you are on the right side of the trade it can be a beautiful thing, but if you are short it is your worst nightmare. Still, with the right stop-loss, this trade could easily have netted over a +40 percent return in three months. Even a shorter-term hold of four weeks would have netted a +25 percent return on equity, and in a down market no less. That truly is *trend trading for a living*!

Sometimes it can be scary to short a stock already trading at new near-term lows. It is counterintuitive to the "buy low, sell high" mentality. One exercise I find helpful is to turn the chart I am looking at upside down, and then ask: "Would I buy this stock?" If yes, then turn the chart right side up again and short the heck out of it! To turn a chart upside down, or invert it, is easy with Stockcharts.com: simply type "$ONE" before the symbol as you input it.

The Rising Wedge Breakdown

Market Type   This setup is best used in:

- Bullish: weakly trending markets
- Bullish: strongly trending markets
- Range-bound markets

Characteristics   This final setup is similar but not identical to the bullish base breakout mentioned previously. Like its bullish cousin, this setup can be traded in a variety of markets. It is also a contrarian play. Here we are looking for a stock that is in an uptrend but is ready to fall out of that trend in dramatic fashion. The *wedge* is created when the oscillations of the uptrend get narrower and narrower. To render the setup valid, we need to see indicators tell us two things about price behavior within the wedge: its momentum has to be slowing down and there needs to be evidence that shares are being distributed (sold) more than accumulated (bought). While longer holds of this setup can return spectacular gains, there is often a quick burst of selling activity at the point of breakdown that can bring gains of +10 percent or more within a few days, making this an ideal trend trade setup.

Key Indicators   This setup relies on a price pattern (*rising wedge*) combined with two technical indicators: MACD and on balance volume (OBV). Here are the specifics:

- First, the stock must be clearly seen to be in an uptrend of some kind, either strong or weak (see preceding definition).
- Second, the up and down swings of the uptrend must be trading within a narrower and narrower range. When this happens, price prints a pattern called a wedge. You can better visualize the wedge by drawing in support and resistance trendlines under the bottoms of lows and over the tops of highs in the uptrend. To qualify as a wedge, you must have at least three price point touches (not high or low pivots, but simply intraday touches) at each trendline, and the more touches, the better.
    - Rising wedges can have a flat top like the ascending triangle shown in Figure 10.11.
    - Or they can look like the pattern shown in Figure 10.12, where both trendlines are rising.
- Once we have identified a wedge pattern in an uptrending stock, we need to confirm that it is a bearish rising wedge. We do this by referring to two technical indicators: MACD and OBV.

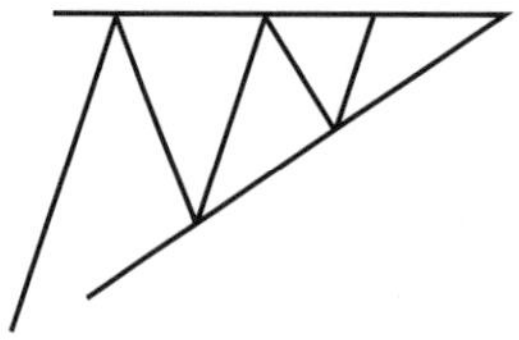

Figure 10.11   Ascending triangle wedge pattern.

Figure 10.12   Rising triangle wedge pattern.

- MACD must be making a series of lower highs while price is within the wedge (price may or may not be making lower highs).
- OBV must fall below a trendline placed under the lows of the indicator.
- *Sell short signal:* A sell short signal is triggered in a rising wedge at the first red or black candle (close is lower than the open) after the candlestick on which the OBV trendline broke to the downside. You can also enter on the day of an OBV break if that candle is red or black.

The Screening Tool   It is not possible to screen for rising wedges using what is commonly available, but the following screen will turn up a few decent candidates among many false hits that can be short-listed for further research. Readers who are more adept at this sort of thing than I am might want to fiddle around with these parameters to make them more robust.

- For the last market close:
- U.S. stocks with . . .
  - 20-day simple moving average of volume for today is greater than 500,000.
  - 60-day simple moving average of close for today is greater than 10.
  - 50-day simple moving average of close for today is greater than 20-day simple moving average of close for today.
  - 50-day simple moving average of close for today

is greater than 50-day simple moving average of
close for 40 days ago.

- Maximum range over 30 days starting today is
  greater than maximum range over 15 days starting today.
- Maximum range over 15 days starting today is
  greater than maximum range over 5 days starting today.
- Daily OBV for today is less than daily OBV for
  40 days ago.
- Daily MACD line (12,26,9) for today is less than
  daily MACD Line (12,26,9) for 40 days ago.
- 50-day simple moving average of close for today
  is greater than 200-day simple moving average
  of close for today.

In the absence of a solid screen, you will just have to
eyeball the charts on your watch list. In fact, this is a better way to go because it allows you to watch a wedge
develop over several days and weeks. That OBV trigger signal is really the key to this setup: if you can get in on the
day that happens, you often will be in at the very start of a
significant trend-down sell-off. The stocks that show up on
the preceding screen most often have already triggered
their OBV trendline signal.

In Figure 10.13, NVDA begins to trade within a narrowing range or wedge just before breaking down. Note
that once we have the two trendlines in place we can clearly
see that the support line is rising at a steeper pace than the
resistance line. The indicators told us ahead of time that

Figure 10.13   NVDA breaks down from a rising wedge pattern.

trouble was ahead, and indeed it was. An entry at the close on the day of the sell short trigger—the break of the OBV trendline—would have returned +30 percent at the maximum extension of the trade in just about four weeks. Note, too, that the sell short trigger occurred prior to price breaking down out of the wedge pattern.

In Figure 10.14, CSCO throws up a rising wedge breakdown signal following a bullish gap up in a strong

Figure 10.14   CSCO triggers OBV sell signal in rising wedge.

uptrend. Even though the price has not yet closed below the wedge, this is still a valid signal and can be entered on the close of the trigger day at a price of 20.75. Note the bearish candle on the trigger day and the bearish divergence seen in the MACD indicator.

That wedge breakdown sell trigger signaled the end to CSCO's uptrend. After price took a few sessions to clear the lower edge of the trendline, it was a slow and steady drop over the next two months to hit a closing low of 17.24,

Figure 10.15   CSCO rising wedge breakdown setup.

for a nice return of +17 percent. Note how the wedge breakout triggered the transition from a strong uptrend to a strong downtrend in CSCO shares in Figure 10.15.

THE FINAL SCREENING PROCESS

Okay, so you've eyeballed all your charts, run your special screens, and now you have a shortlist of stocks to consider either buying long or selling short. The next thing you need to do is whittle this list of possible plays down to only the most highly qualified, most riskworthy candidates, which you will monitor the next trading day for entries. Input each stock into your Stockcharts.com chart setup with all the indicators I've listed in the aforementioned setups. Make sure the chart is large enough to get a good, clear picture of at least six months of daily data. You then put each setup through a series of tests. Do not—I repeat, *do not*—be tempted to skip this further testing. It is tedious and sometimes yields few results, but it is absolutely essential if you want to streamline your shortlist down to the one or two best possible trades for the day. In this process you are going from your B-list to your A-list of stocks. This last step is key to putting the greatest number of odds on your side.

Here is how you would further test or screen your shortlists per the various setups we have just discussed.

Bullish Setups

The pullback: *You will favor stocks where . . .*

- Volume on the dip to support is lower than average.
- There is no close during the dip under the 50 MA.
- The trendline supporting the uptrend has not been violated.
- There is no bearish divergence seen in any of the indicators.
- Price has not put in a double top formation (two equal price highs) on the daily chart.
- The weekly chart shows that price is not trading

just under a major weekly moving average (like the 50 MA or 200 MA).
- Earnings are set to be announced at least two weeks after entry (to avoid unnecessary volatility).

The coiled spring: You will favor stocks where . . .

- Volume in the coil is lower than average.
- The coil is longer than 7 candles but not longer than 15 candles.
- There is no close in the coil under the 50 MA.
- There are more green candles (close higher than the open) in the coil than red candles (close lower than the open).
- At least two of the RSI, CCI and OBV are rising during the coil.
- The weekly chart shows that price is not trading just under a major weekly moving average (like the 50 MA or 200 MA).
- Earnings are set to be announced at least two weeks after entry.

The bullish divergence: *You will favor stocks where . . .*

- You see above-average volume during the last low.
- The last low is near an area of previous price support, long-term trendline support, or major moving average support.
- The divergences on the indicators relative to price are strong (i.e., much lower price low plus much higher indicator low).

- There are more than two indicator divergences.
- The last low is more than 10 percent away from the 20 MA.
- The weekly chart shows that price is not trading just under a major weekly moving average (like the 50 MA or 200 MA).
- Earnings are set to be announced at least two weeks after entry.

The blue sky breakout: You will favor stocks where . . .

- You see above-average volume on the breakout day.
- The breakout high is the highest price for six months or more.
- The breakout follows a period of price consolidation, with several unsuccessful attempts to break to new highs.
- Earnings are set to be announced at least two weeks after entry.

The bullish base breakout: You will favor stocks where . . .

- You see above-average volume on the signal day.
- Price has not yet broken out of the bullish base.
- The base is prolonged beyond the minimum time required.
- There are more green candles in the base than red candles.
- At least two of the RSI, CCI and OBV are rising during the base.

- The weekly chart shows the base lying at or near a major weekly moving average (20, 50, 200).
- Earnings are set to be announced at least two weeks after entry.

Bearish Setups

The relief rally: You will favor stocks where . . .

- Volume on the rally to resistance is lower than average.
- There is no close during the dip above the 50 MA.
- The trendline containing the downtrend has not been violated.
- There is no bullish divergence seen in any of the indicators.
- Price has not printed in a double bottom or inverted head-and-shoulders formation on the daily chart.
- The weekly chart shows that price is not trading just under a major weekly moving average (like the 50 MA or 200 MA).
- Earnings are set to be announced at least two weeks after entry.

The Bearish Divergence: You will favor stocks where . . .

- You see above-average volume during the last high.
- The last high is near an area of previous price resistance.

- The divergences on the indicators relative to price are strong (i.e., much higher price high plus much lower indicator high).
- The divergences on the indicators are strong.
- There are more than two indicator divergences.
- The last high is more than 10 percent away from the 20 MA.
- The weekly chart shows that price is not trading just under a major weekly moving average (like the 50 MA or 200).
- Earnings are set to be announced at least two weeks after entry.

The gap down: You will favor stocks where . . .

- You see above-average volume on the gap down day.
- The high preceding the gap down is at an area of previous price resistance.
- The high preceding the gap down corresponds to bearish divergence on one or more of our primary indicators.
- Earnings are set to be announced at least two weeks after entry.

The blue sea breakdown: You will favor stocks where . . .

- You see above-average volume on the breakdown day.
- The breakdown low is the lowest price for six months or more.

- The breakdown follows a period of price consolidation, with several unsuccessful attempts to break to new lows.
- Earnings are set to be announced at least two weeks after entry.

The rising wedge breakdown: You will favor stocks where . . .

- You see above-average volume on the signal day.
- Price has not yet broken out of the wedge.
- You will favor rising wedges over ascending triangle wedges.
- There are more red candles in the wedge than green candles.
- At least two of the RSI, CCI, and OBV are falling during the wedge.
- The weekly chart shows the wedge lying at or near a major weekly moving average (20, 50, 200).
- Earnings are set to be announced at least two weeks after entry.

This final screening process will force you to focus only on those stocks that have the highest technical merit. This final list is now ready for one last question, and it is an all-important one: *Is the risk/reward ratio worth taking a chance on?*

To calculate a stock's risk/reward ratio, divide the percentage of your expected gain by the percentage of your initial stop-loss. If you plan on trailing a stop-loss (to be explained in the Chapter 11) as the trade moves in your favor, then you will need only a 1.25 ratio or better. For example, if your target price is +10 percent, then you can afford a stop-loss of (8 percent because as the trade moves in your favor, this percentage loss gets smaller and smaller, and your risk/reward ratio becomes more favorable. The best risk/reward scenarios, however, start at 2.0 or better. Any setup that cannot predict at least a 10 percent return before running into significant resistance should be scratched.

One final note: Don't be afraid to say, even after several hours of hard work, that you simply do not have any setups that have either enough technical merit or a high enough risk/reward ratio to warrant your investment. As Donald Trump says, "Sometimes the best investments are the ones you don't make." Not that we need to take investment advice from The Donald, but the point is well taken: it is best to stand aside and see what the next day's trading offers than to risk good money in less-than-optimal trades.

ENTRIES AND EXITS

Before going further, let me take a moment here to remind you of what was written earlier about trading psychology. There I listed several major resources that will help traders work through the emotional and temperamental issues that can so often undermine even the most robust trading systems. If you skipped over that section, and if you (like me) struggle with strictly following the trading plan you have laid out, then I suggest you go back and read through that section of the book again. Study one or more of the resources listed there. Spend a week on your emotional control and you will go far toward establishing a lifetime of profitable trading.

ENTERING THE TRADE

If you find a stock that satisfies all the requirements of a particular setup, and it has passed your further screening process and presents a favorable risk/reward ratio, then entering that trade is merely a matter of picking the best entry price and setting an order with the broker for that price. In every case for all the setups, I recommend the following as the most reasonable and profitable way to pick the best entry price.

For Long Setups

- Once all your requirements for a valid entry have been satisfied on the chart, enter the trade on a stop order set at either $0.02 (for slower-moving stocks) or $0.05 (for faster-moving stocks) above the intraday high of the previous trading day.
- If the stock gaps up above this buy point, then set a limit order for that price and wait for the price to come back down. If it never hits this buy price, then consider the trade a scratch and move on.

For Short Setups

- Once all your requirements for a valid entry have been satisfied on the chart, enter the trade on a stop order to sell at either $0.02 (for slower-moving stocks) or $0.05 (for faster-moving stocks) below the intraday low of the previous trading day.
- If the stock gaps down below this sell short point, then set a limit order for that price and wait for the price to come back up. If it never hits this sell short price, then either pay up for your shares or consider the trade a scratch and move on.

Let me add to that last note an important principle: the entry is the least important part of trading. Too many traders angst out over shaving a penny or two off their entry price. I've seen traders abandon excellent, extremely profitable setups simply because they were afraid of paying up a nickel for their shares. So don't worry about the entry. If you've got a great setup and your entry price is not hit by the end of the day, don't skimp. Pay up and adjust your stop and target accordingly.

Entering the trade is the easy part. Knowing when to exit, now that is hard. Not only is it hard, but for most mortals it is close to impossible to exit a trade anywhere near the right time. When a trade goes against us, we either panic and sell too soon or entertain irrational hopes and hold on too long. When a trade moves in our favor, we either exit too soon out of fear or hang on too long out of greed. The true geniuses of trading, the masters of the mouse who can turn the chaotic noise of the markets into profitable events, are all extremely proficient at knowing when to exit trades.

That kind of genius, that sixth sense that seems to know intuitively just when a price will pivot, is probably a birthright, a divine gift. For the rest of us, we need hard-and-fast rules; rules that, if followed, will restrain our emotions and rational minds long enough to keep us from making the kind of embarrassing clown trades I described in the Introduction. In the following section I outline the rules. There are several exit strategies suggested here. Try each one for yourself to determine which strategy best fits your trading style.

STOP-LOSSES

Once you are in a trade, you will need to put into action your exit strategy. That strategy must take into account two different possibilities: the trade goes against you and you need to exit in order to cut your loss short, or the trade goes in your favor and you need to bank the profit before, inevitably, the momentum fades. In this section we will deal with the first of these two possibilities: how to manage losses.

Remember, we are not position traders and not buy-and-holders. Trend trading is not about trying to grab the full move of a stock's price, only the "meat" of the current trend. We want a high percentage of wins (at least +60 percent, but up to +80 percent is possible with some systems and in certain market conditions), small losses, and no regrets about banking small profits. Obviously, we want our profits to run, but we are quick on the trigger to bank those profits when they begin to dwindle (and they nearly always will if you hold long enough). The way we minimize our losses in the event a trade turns against us is to set a *stop-loss*.

Every trade you put on needs to have an exact price at which you will *definitely* sell it in the event the trade goes against you. This is what we call a stop-loss: a specified exit you will take *no matter what* in order to cut your losses. One more time: every trade needs a stop-loss, and a stop-loss is that exact price (not a notional, in-your-head price "area"—give me a break!) at which you will close the position in the event of a loss or decrease in profit.

I teach my students four different methods for setting stop-losses. The method that works best for you depends on the kind of trader you are, your trading experience, your chart-reading experience, your tolerance for risk, and so on. I recommend experimenting with these four types of stops to see which is most profitable for you. Remember, the only wrong way to put on a stop-loss is to put on no stop-loss. The four stop-loss methods are:

- A percentage stop-loss
- A price pattern stop-loss
- An average true range stop-loss
- A parabolic SAR stop-loss

Percentage Stop-Loss

The *percentage stop-loss* is the easiest to set. It works this way: to set a stop-loss, simply calculate a percentage loss from your point of entry and set the stop at that price. In trend trading, your expected percentage return varies from stock to stock, depending on the issue's volatility and the pattern or setup you are trading. In most cases, however, due to the relatively short-term nature of these trades, you will want to set a stop-loss no greater than −8 percent on any given trade no matter what you expect to gain from a successful completion of the trade. You should move this stop at the end of each day, as long as the trade moves in your favor, recalculating the percentage stop from the current closing price. Some online brokerages will allow for a *trailing stop*, which will automatically recalculate your stop-loss at every new intraday high (if long) or low (if short), or at every new closing price if you select that option.

Price Pattern Stop-Loss

A more sophisticated stop-loss, and the one I use myself, is the *price pattern stop-loss*: here we want to look for an area on the chart of nearby price support (if long) or resistance

orice were to violate that area would sig-
 is not likely to work out. Price support
 come in the form of a major moving
 previous price reversal, or a trendline.
..uers familiar with Bollinger Bands or other forms of standard deviation envelopes can also use those tools to set price pattern stops.

The price pattern stop-loss is a more reasonable way to apply stop-losses in that, instead of relying on an arbitrary distance away from the entry price, it uses a distance suggested by the price action of the stock itself. Furthermore, a price pattern stop gives you a quick read on the risk/reward ratio. Say, for example, your stock is in a strong uptrend and has pulled back to the 50 MA and then triggered an entry signal only 3 percent above that MA, and at the same time you calculate a target price of 12 percent. This would prove to be an excellent risk/reward entry. But in every case, I recommend not risking more than an 8 percent loss on any given trade. In most trades you should set a stop-loss at something more like 5 to 6 percent. The average loss in our Swing Trade Newsletter, for example, is 4.76 percent. Leave it to the investors and position traders to take the double-digit losses!

Average True Range (ATR)

A third way to calculate a stop-loss is to use the *average true range* (ATR) of the stock. The "R" in ATR stands for the range of intraday movement a stock makes from its intraday high to its intraday low; the "T" is there because this calculation also includes the previous day's closing price, thus incorporating any overnight gap; and the "A" signifies that a running average of these figures is what makes up the indicator's end value. The ATR is a measurement of the intraday volatility of the stock. As shares tend to trade within a larger intraday range, ATR moves up. As price consolidates and the intraday moves tighten, ATR moves down. Using ATR to set your stop-loss means you are correlating the amount you are willing to lose with the stock's volatility: the greater the volatility, the greater the potential reward, but also the greater the potential loss.

Most charting packages will calculate ATR for you. The default periodicity for the ATR is usually set at 14, which works just fine. Double the ATR value and in most cases you have a reasonable place to set a stop-loss. If that figure is more than 8 percent from the entry price, the stock may be too volatile for a swing trade and should either be entered very lightly with a tighter stop or not entered at all. The ATR has the added advantage of giving you a valuable tool for position sizing, and it is used in a variety of formulas by fund managers seeking to reduce risk in their portfolios.

Parabolic SAR Stop

A fourth and final way to input a stop-loss, the *parabolic SAR stop-loss*, can also be done with your charting package. Most charting packages will allow you to overlay a parabolic SAR (stop and reverse) indicator on the price chart. This indicator was developed by Welles Wilder as a means of trading volatile stocks in a stop-and-reverse fashion: if you were stopped out long, you would immediately go short, and vice versa. The indicator doesn't work that well on most stocks as an SAR entry system, but it is a handy tool for setting stop exits. The SAR overlay consists of a series of dots under each day's candlestick. Some lie under price lows and some lie above price highs. As the stock moves up and down, these dots change location. They even change if the stock trades flat. The parabolic SAR is designed as both a price and a time stop: if the trade goes nowhere, or even if it goes against you, your stop-loss tightens up regardless—hence, the parabolic effect of the tool.

Your charting package will tell you the value of the current day's SAR, so that value is then your stop price. Figure 11.1 is an example of a chart with the parabolic SAR overlay on it (MRVL). You can see that the SAR nicely catches the major trends, but it loses money during choppier market moves.

HOW TO BANK YOUR PROFITS

The second possibility with your open position occurs when the trade moves in your favor. Here you are left with the more pleasurable but admittedly very difficult decision of choosing when to exit the trade with the greatest amount of profit. Many traders struggle more with selling too early than with cutting losses.

I teach my students four different methods for taking profits on their trades. Again, the method that works best for you depends on the kind of trader you are, your trading experience, your chart-reading experience, your

Figure 11.1   MRVL showing parabolic SAR stop points.

tolerance for risk, and so on. I recommend experimenting with these four types of profit exits and see which works best for you. Remember, no one goes broke taking profits. The four profit exit methods we will cover here are:

- A percentage profit exit
- A price support or resistance profit exit
- An average true range profit exit
- The trailing stop profit exit

Percentage Profit Exit

The simplest exit strategy is to use a *percentage profit exit*. Here you should place a profit target limit order to close the trade at a percentage removed from your entry price that is 1.5 to 2.0 times that of your stop-loss. For example, if you have set a −5.0 percent stop-loss, then you would set your profit limit order somewhere between +7.5 and +10.0 percent. Your stop-loss order may change as the stock moves in your favor, but you must keep your profit limit order in place at all times. The trade is considered closed when either one or the other is hit and executes. With the kind of volatile, high-beta stocks we screen for, this usually happens within a few days.

Price Resistance or Price Support Exit

A more sophisticated way of setting a profit limit order is to look for an area of nearby *price resistance* (if long) or *price support* (if short) such that if price were to reach that area it would likely attract the wrong kind of crowd (sellers pouncing at resistance or buyers gathering shares at support). Price support or resistance can come in the form of a major moving average, an area of previous price reversal, or a trendline. Traders familiar with Bollinger Bands or other forms of standard deviation envelopes can also use those tools to set price pattern stops. This is a more reasonable way to approach profit limits, and it takes advantage of your chart-reading skills.

Average True Range Profit Exit

A third way to calculate your exit target is to use an *average true range profit exit*. To calculate this, simply multiply your ATR by 3, assuming you set your stop at 2*ATR. So say, for example, you are trading RIMM long, which is currently being offered at 96.82 with an ATR of 3.25. If your entry price was 96.00, say, you would then set your stop-loss at $96.00 - (2 \times 3.25)$, or 89.50, and your target limit order at $96.00 + (3 \times 3.25)$, or 105.75.

Trailing Stop Profit Exit

The fourth and final way to bank your profits, and the way I normally use, is simply to take your stop-loss and move it in response to any positive movement in your position (up for longs, down for shorts) on a closing basis. This is called *a trailing stop exit*, and studies show it is by far the most profitable. Why is this? Because it follows the age-old trader's dictum: "Let your winners run." Setting specific profit targets is often the favored choice for trend trading because it keeps your turnover of trades flowing smoothly. It is the right choice if you need your trading account to produce a steady cash flow in order to pay your bills. The problem with using profit targets, however, is that you then miss out on those few big runs that, in themselves, can be all the fuel you need to get your account into the big leagues. In fact, you can take losses in the majority of your trades, but if you cut them short and let your winners run, those two or three huge winners you are bound to get each year can keep you at the trading game a long, long time.

Read the *Market Wizards* stories: nearly every trader there looks back on one or two huge winners that propelled them from amateur wannabes into the professional trading arena. So if you are not sure where to place a profit target, or you think your position could be the next Google, hold on to it for a while with a trailing stop-loss and let the market take you out of the trade.

REAL-TIME TRADING

In this chapter you have an account of everything you need to know to execute profitable trend trades. What is not here, and indeed cannot be here, is perhaps the most important part of trend trading: real-time experience. There is no substitute for the countless hours it will take to put this knowledge into practice in a way that will lead you to find technically sound trading setups, make consistently profitable trades, take reasonably small losses, and ultimately ramp up your trading account to new highs. To put into practice what you have learned in this chapter, I suggest you take the following action steps:

1. *Read this chapter at least twice.* We all read through our prejudices, and these may cause you to overlook important bits of information. Go back over this material to be sure to catch items you may have missed on the first reading.

2. *Spend several trading days just eyeballing your watch lists.* There is no substitute for putting in hours of chart reading for the setups we teach in this book. You will need to so internalize these setups that they become second nature to you. You need to gain that intuitive sense for stocks that look somewhat like a particular setup but have other issues going on that likely would weigh against the setup, and that intuitive sense for a setup that is just so outrageously perfect that you can hardly wait to enter your position the next day.

3. *Give serious thought to position sizing.* This could constitute an entire chapter by itself, but instead of boring you with my theories let me suggest that you read Chapter 12 of Van Tharp's book *Trade Your*

Way to Financial Freedom. Short of that, I always
recommend that my students divide their accounts
into equal monetary amounts and put no more than
that amount into each trade. When you are first
starting out as a trend trader, you should go very
lightly into your trades (dividing by 10 ought to
work). You can increase your size as you gain
more experience. It is also not a bad idea to scale
back on size during a losing streak and increase
in size during a winning streak. That may seem
counterintuitive, but in the game of trading, losing
tends to beget more losing and winning tends to
beget more winning.

TREND TRADING
WITH OPTIONS

OPTIONS BASICS

L ET'S look at another form of trend trading using a different asset class: stock options. Options will add a great deal of flexibility to your trend trading. Don't like the risk in a certain setup, but you really like the chart? Trade the options instead. Don't have much cash on hand, but you want to get in on a predicted move in Google (currently trading well over $500 per share)? Buy the options for a lot less. Do you have a large amount of profit in your open positions, and you fear the markets are about to reverse? Add some price insurance—with options. Want to profit from the huge moves that take place during earnings season but don't want to risk being on the wrong side? You can do that too—with (you guessed it!) options. So, you may be asking, what the heck are options?

WHAT ARE OPTIONS?

Options are traded just like stocks. You can either buy them in the hope that they will rise in price or sell them short (this is also called *writing* an option) in the hope that they will fall in price. There are only two kinds of stock options: calls and puts. Call options tend to rise in price as the stock price rises. Put options tend to rise in price as the stock price falls. So both the buyer of a call option and the writer of a put option, generally, are bullish on the stock. And both the writer of a call option and the buyer of a put option, generally, are bearish on the stock.

Option buyers have rights, and option writers have obligations. Option buyers have the right, but not the obligation, to buy (if a call is bought) or sell (if a put is bought) the underlying stock at a specified price. This right remains in place until the option expires. Each option contract you purchase will have a specified expiration month associated with it. Options expire on the third Friday of their expiration month. Option writers have the obligation to sell (if a call is sold short) or buy (if a put is sold short) the underlying stock at a specified price. This obligation remains in place until the option expires.

There are no margin requirements if you want to purchase an option because your risk is limited to the price of the option. An option purchase requires the account to be debited in the amount of the option's purchase price, or *premium*. Option writers, on the other hand, receive a credit to their account in the amount of the option's premium for selling that option. They get to keep this amount if the option expires worthless on its expiration date. However, since option sellers also have an obligation to buy (put) or sell (call) the underlying stock if their option is exercised by the person they sold their option to (the *assigned option holder*), they assume a risk greater than the amount of the price of the option. Therefore, writing an option always requires the use of a margin account. Not all brokers allow for the writing or selling of options unless the writer or seller also owns shares of the underlying stock.

STOCK OPTIONS TERMINOLOGY

To trade options, you must be acquainted with the terminology of the options market. I've provided here a list of the most commonly used terms associated with buying and selling stock options.

At-the-Money
An option is at-the-money if the market price of the underlying interest is at or near the underlying stock price.

Generally, at-the-money options cost more than out-of-the-money options.

Buy to Close
Buying to close is when you buy a contract that you are currently short.

Buy to Open
Buying to open a position is when you buy a contract that you don't already own.

Call Option
A call option is a contract that gives the holder the right to buy the underlying for the strike price anytime until expiry.

Delta

There are several Greek letter symbols used in options terminology that refer to changes in an option's premium. The most important of these for our purposes is *delta*.

Delta refers to a ratio between option premium and stock price. This relationship is not normally a 1:1 ratio. Most often it is around 0.5:1 (and often less than that). In other words, if the delta for an option is 0.5, then for every $1 move in the stock, there is a corresponding $0.50 move in the option premium. That may make it seem like options are not as good a deal as stocks, but the fact that options are leveraged by price—it takes a lot less money to control 100 shares buying the options rather than the shares—makes them very attractive despite the delta ratio.

There is some good news regarding delta: it changes as the stock price moves more and more in-the-money. Usually, at the strike price delta is around 0.5. Deep in-the-money options, however, can move at closer to a 1:1 ratio. The opposite is true as well: if the stock moves away from the strike price and out of the money, delta tends to decrease. This factor alone—the delta factor—makes options very attractive for trend trading: as a position moves in our favor, our options increase in value at a faster and faster rate, but as a position moves against us, they decrease in value at a slower and slower rate.

Exercise Style

- **American Style:** American-style options can be exercised anytime until expiry.
- **European Style:** European-style options can be exercised only on expiry (not before).

Exercise and Assignment

Exercise is when the option holder decides to use the option to buy or sell the underlying stock at the strike price. *Assignment* is when an option seller (called the *writer* of an option) is required to buy or sell the underlying stock due to the obligation from writing the option. An option holder exercising an option will cause an option writer to be assigned.

Expiration Date

A stock option expires by the market's close on the third Friday of the expiration month. All listed options have options available for the current month and the next month as well as specific future months. Each stock has a corresponding cycle of months that they offer options in. There are three fixed expiration cycles available. They are as follows:

1. January, April, July, and October

2. February, May, August, and November

3. March, June, September, and December

The date the option expires is referred to as the *expiration date*.

Holder

The holder is the person who bought an option contract. People who buy an option they previously wrote are not holders, they are just closing an existing position. Option holders are said to be *long* the option they bought.

In-the-Money

- *Call options:* The underlying stock price is above the option strike price.
- *Put options:* The underlying stock price is below the option strike price.
- *Note:* All options with intrinsic value are in-the-money.

Generally, in-the-money options cost more to purchase than at-the-money options.

Intrinsic Value

Intrinsic value is the portion of an options premium that is attributed to the value that could currently be realized by exercising and simultaneously closing out the position in the open market.

Long

If you own a security or stock option, you are said to be *long* that security or option.

Out-of-the-Money

- *Call options:* The underlying stock price is below the option strike price.
- *Put options:* The underlying stock price is above the option strike price.

Premium

A premium is the price that is paid for an option contract.

An option's premium is determined by a number of factors including, but not limited to, the current price of the underlying asset, the strike price of the option, the time remaining until expiration (time value), and the volatility of the stock. An option premium is priced on a per-share basis. Each option on a stock corresponds to 100 shares. Therefore, if the premium of an option is priced at 2.50, the total cost for that option would be $250 per contract (2.50 premium × 100 shares per contract). Buying an option creates a debit in the amount of the option's total cost to the buyer's trading account. Writing or selling short an option creates a credit in the amount of the option's total cost to the seller's trading account.

Put Option

A put option is a contract that gives the holder the right to sell the underlying for the strike price anytime until expiry.

Sell to Close

Selling to close is selling a contract you currently own.

Short

If you sell a security or stock option you didn't already own, you are said to be *short* that security or option.

Time Value

The time remaining until expiration of a purchased option has a monetary value in options trading. This value is called the option's *time value*. Time value increases the further away from expiration the option is, and it decreases as the option moves closer to expiration. The rate of this decrease changes exponentially over time, so as an option moves closer and closer to expiration, the option's time value decreases at a faster and faster rate. On the day of expiration, options possess no time value whatsoever.

Strike Price (Exercise Price)

The strike price is the price that the underlying asset will be bought or sold at if an option contract is exercised.

Options are available in several strike prices above and below the current price of the underlying asset. Stocks priced below $25 per share usually have strike prices at intervals of $2.50. Stocks priced over $25 usually have strike prices at $5 intervals.

Underlying

The underlying is something that an option contract is based on. This could be a stock, an index, a foreign currency, an interest rate, or a futures contract. The underlying is commonly referred to as the *underlying interest*, *underlying asset*, *underlying security*, or *underlying stock*.

Writer

A writer is someone who sold an option contract to open a position. The writer is the person who is taking on the risk (underwriting the risk). People who sell an options contract they already own are not writers, they are just closing an existing position. Option writers are said to be *short* the option they wrote.

Write (Sell to Open)

Selling to open is selling short an options contract that you don't already own. The writer is the person taking on the risk (underwriting the risk). People who sell an options contract they already own are not writers, they are just closing an existing position. Option writers are said to be *short* the option they wrote.

SUMMARY OF HOW OPTIONS WORK

- Stock options give you the right to buy or sell an underlying stock.
- If you buy an option, you are not obligated to buy or sell the underlying stock; you simply have the right to do so.
- If you sell an option and the option is exercised, you are obligated to deliver the underlying stock (if you bought a call) or take delivery of the underlying stock (if you bought a put) at the strike price of the option, regardless of the current price of the underlying stock.
- Options are good for a specified period of time, after which they expire and you lose your right to buy or sell the underlying instrument at the specified price.
- Options when bought are done so at a debit to the buyer.
- Options when sold are done so by giving a credit to the seller.
- Options are available in several strike prices representing the price of the underlying instrument.
- The cost of an option is referred to as the option *premium*. The price reflects a variety of factors

including the current price of the underlying stock, the strike price of the option, the time remaining until expiration, and volatility.
- Options are not available on every stock. There are approximately 2,200 stocks with tradable options. Each stock option represents 100 shares of a company's stock.

ADVANTAGES OF OPTIONS

Options are the most versatile trading instruments available. They can, for example, be traded on a wide variety of instruments, including stocks, stock indexes, exchange-traded funds (like the QQQQ), commodities, currencies, and bonds. Options on all these instruments function in exactly the same way as described previously. Our focus here, however, will be on stock options.

Options are also versatile because they can be used for a larger variety of reasons than simple stocks.

- *Options are used to hedge against risk.*

If you have 1,000 shares of IBM, for example, and suspect that the stock might be in for a drawdown, you can buy 10 put options (or sell 10 calls), which would increase in value in that event. Once the sell-off was over, you could then sell the puts for a profit against the loss suffered in the stock. The effect is twofold: you are partially protected against a loss in the stock, and the profit from the option sale serves to lower the entry cost of the IBM stock.

- *Options can also be used to profit from periods when the markets are volatile and unpredictable.*

There are certain market-neutral strategies using options that take advantage of the fact that options tend to gain in value at an increasing rate as a stock moves favorably, but decrease in value at a decreasing rate as a stock moves unfavorably. This is the aforementioned *delta* factor of an option, and it can yield incredibly consistent gains if played wisely. If, for example, one expects RIMM to move wildly on its earnings announcement, but you are not sure whether that move will be up or down, you can purchase both a call and a put on RIMM. If on the day of the announcement RIMM trades up strongly, you can sell the put for a loss and hold the call for the gain. Because of the delta factor, the put should decrease in value at a rate slower than the increase in value of the call option. This is a profitable variance that can be exploited again and again, particularly during earnings season. We will teach you how to implement this strategy later.

- *Options give the smaller account trader an incredible amount of leverage with which to play higher-priced stocks.*

By buying a call or put instead of the actual stock, a trader with only a couple thousand dollars to trade can still control round lots of the stock instead of having to purchase odd lots (less than 100 shares). He or she can take full positions in some of the higher-priced stocks, the big movers, when normally the smaller trading capital would have prohibited it. With options, a smaller account trader can take multiple positions without tying up all his or her cash.

But the primary advantage of stock options versus simple stocks is *leverage*. Leverage is here defined as the advantage gained by the investor who can make a small amount of money do the work of a much larger amount. In stock options, you can frequently put yourself in a situation where every $1 invested in options is doing work equivalent to $10 or more invested in stocks.

Let's give a real-world example. Let's say I wanted to buy 500 shares of EBAY because I think it is going to go up over the next few weeks. Currently EBAY is trading at about $40 per share. So those 500 shares of EBAY are going to cost me $20,000. Let's also say that I am right: over the next month, EBAY goes to $50. My 500 shares are now worth $25,000. I have made a profit of: $5,000, or +25 percent on my original investment, less commissions. Here is a summary of my stock trade:

- Buy 500 shares EBAY @ $40: cost $20,000
- Stock goes to $50: profit $5,000, or +25 percent

Anytime you can bank a 25 percent gain in a month, you've made a nice trade.

But now let's say, instead of buying the stock outright, I purchased call options on the stock instead. If EBAY is trading at $40, and I think it is going to go up, I would want to buy calls at the 40 strike at least two months out (to give my trade time to mature). Currently the premium on these options is about 4.00, or a cost of $400 per contract. I'm going to buy five contracts at a cost of $2,000. Again, I'm right, and EBAY rockets to $50. At a delta of 0.5, which then increases to about 0.7 as the calls move from being *at-the-money* to being *in-the-money*, the premium on my calls increases from 4.00 to about 10.00. Those five options are now worth $5,000. I have made a profit of $3,000 less commissions. While this is less than the profit made with the stock purchase, it represents an overall gain of an astonishing +150 percent. To put this into perspective: if I had put the same amount of money into the options as I had put into the stock ($20,000), I could have bought 50 calls. Those 50 calls would have risen to a premium value of $50,000, or a net profit of $30,000 versus the $5,000 I made trading the stock. That's 600 percent leverage. That's what I'm talking about with options. Leverage, baby, leverage!

So to summarize:

- Buy 5 EBAY 40 calls @ $400: total cost = $2,000
- Stock goes to $50: profit = $3,000, or +150 percent

But what happens if EBAY does not move in my expected direction? If instead of shooting up $10, it drops $10? What happens to my investment then? Well, if I had simply bought 500 shares of the stock, I would be down $5,000. My $20,000 investment would now be worth only $15,000, for a loss of 25 percent. But if I had bought five call contracts instead of the stock, I would also be down, but not as much. Again, delta works in our favor in the event of a loss. As EBAY's stock price moves against us, and our options go further and further out-of-the-money, the rate of decrease in the premium value slows down. I will lose some time value during the days of EBAY's sell-off, but the overall amount of loss in premium tends to decrease relative to the loss in the underlying stock. This means that buying the options provides less risk than owning the stock. For example:

- EBAY goes from $40 to $30 = $5,000 loss on stock trade.
- *But:* My call options go from 4.00 to 2.00 = $1,000 loss on the options trade (compare this to a $3,000 gain if the stock makes the same 10-point move to the upside).
- *So: The options risk/reward ratio is 3.0 times greater than the stock purchase, thanks to the power of delta.*

There are several other advantages to the purchase of stock options versus the purchase of the underlying stock. For one, there is no uptick rule when you want to profit from a stock's sell-off. If you short a stock, normally you must wait for a bid uptick before you can enter the position. Not so with options. You simply buy the put at the offer price. There is no need for an uptick.

With puts, there are no dividends and margin interest to pay. If you short the stock, however, you will be charged interest on 50 percent of your investment (margin fee), and you will also be charged for any payable dividend if there is one.

DISADVANTAGES OF OPTIONS

There are some disadvantages with options that should be pointed out, before anyone thinks they have found the ideal trading vehicle.

- *Time value decay:* Options lose value as they approach expiration, and there is nothing you can do to stop it.
- *The rate of time value decay increases over time:* the closer the option gets to expiration, the faster the decay-see Figure 12.1.
- *Full loss of investment:* If the trade goes against you and you hold the option to expiration (which we caution strongly against in any case), your option will expire worthless.
  - This means you will have to reduce your per-trade investment size, thus reducing your overall gains.
  - It also makes compounding gains more difficult, since 100 percent compounding can lead to irreparable damage if you take a large loss.
- *With options there is no pre- or postmarket trading available:* if you see bad news come out overnight and you own calls, there is nothing you can do about it until the next trading day.
- *There is normally less liquidity in options than in stocks:* Some out-of-the-money options do not trade every day.
  - In general, the more liquid a stock is, and the closer to being at-the-money the option strike is, the more liquid the option will be.

- *There are larger spreads between bid and ask.*
  - In well-traded stocks, the spread on the stock option is usually 0.10 to 0.20.
  - In less liquid stocks, the spread can be 0.40 or more.
- *Options cannot be traded in some IRAs.*
  - Some IRAs restrict options trading to purchase only and forbid the writing of options.

Figure 12.1 is a clear, visual example of the exponential increase in the rate of time value decay as an option approaches its maturity at expiration. This fact increases the risk value of options as they are held over time: if the underlying stock does not move in a favorable direction within a

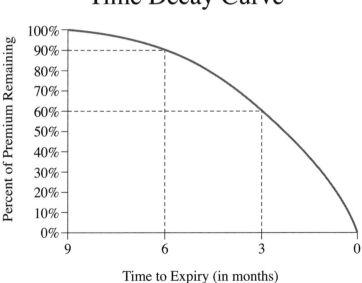

Figure 12.1   Time decay curve.

short period of time following the option's purchase, the chances of that option becoming profitable decrease; the longer the delay, the less likely the chance for profit.

BASIC OPTIONS PARAMETERS

Option contracts possess four identifiers: the underlying, the expiration month, the strike price, and the type.

- The *underlying* = what market the option represents (stock, index, etc.)
- *Expiration date* = the third Friday of the month in which the option expires
- *Strike price* = the price at which the option owner has the right (not the obligation) to purchase the underlying

Options are classified as being *in-the-money* (ITM), *at-the-money* (ATM), or *out-of-the-money* (OTM).

- ITM = the call strike price is less than the underlying price; the put strike price is greater than the underlying price.
- ATM = the call/put strike price is the same as the underlying price.
- OTM = the call strike price is greater than the underlying price; the put strike price is less than the underlying price.

Type = calls or puts. There are only two types of options: *calls* and *puts* (see Figures 12.2 and 12.3).

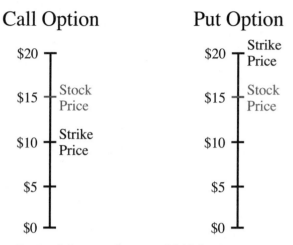

Both of these options are $5.00 in-the-money.

Figure 12.2 ITM options pricing.

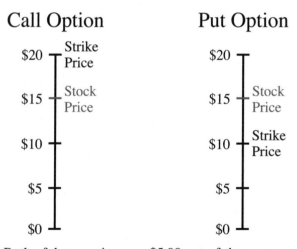

Both of these options are $5.00 out-of-the-money.

Figure 12.3 OTM options pricing.

- A *call option* gives the option buyer the right, but not the obligation, to purchase the underlying market (100 shares per option contract on stock) at a specified price (the strike price) at any time between option purchase and option expiration.
  - Calls bought make money as the market goes up.
  - Calls sold or written make money as the market goes down or stays flat.
- A *put option* gives the option buyer the right, but not the obligation, to sell the underlying market (100 shares per option contract on stock) at a specified price (the strike price) at any time between now and option expiration.
  - Puts bought make money as the market goes down.
  - Puts sold or written make money as the market goes down or stays flat.

Options have two kinds of value, which combine to make the *premium* you must pay to own them:

- *Intrinsic value* (IV) is a function of a variety of factors including the price of the underlying; IV increases as the option moves further in-the-money; IV becomes 0 once an option is out-of-the-money.
- *Time value* (TV) decreases as the option moves closer to expiration; TV becomes 0 at expiration.

Example 1
EBAY Oct 45 calls (EBAY was currently trading in July at $40).

- Option was trading at 4.00 ($400 per contract).
- IV = $0; TV = $4.00.

Example 2
EBAY Oct 35 calls (EBAY was currently trading in July at $40).

- Option trading at 8.00 ($800 per contract).
- IV = $3.00; TV = $5.00.

Note: The volatility of the underlying stock affects time value:

- Decreased volatility = lowered TV.
- Increased volatility = increased TV.

DR. STOXX'S RULES FOR TRADING STOCK OPTIONS

In this section I am going to outline the basic rules I use for trading options on our Befriend the Trend Trading trend trade picks. Many of our newsletter subscribers use options on our picks with truly incredible results. Some use options exclusively and so do not trade those picks whose options do not meet the criteria outlined here. Others use options when the price of the underlying stock is too high for their accounts. Either way, you will learn here how to trend-trade stock options with the least amount of risk.

If you are already a successful trend trader, then you will have no problem at all becoming a successful options trader. Simply follow the rules as I've outlined them here. Remember, these rules are *not* optional. If you want long-term trading success with options, you *must* follow these rules to the letter. You have no choice. Due to their leverage, you cannot trade options in the same way you trade stocks. It may work in the short term, but longer term, you will wipe out your account. Please do not skip this section. Read these rules carefully, write up a brief summary of them in your own words, and post them next to your trading computer.

1. *Never buy options with less than one month to expiration unless they are to be used for day trading.*
   - In this way you avoid the worst period for time value decay and thus take some of the risk out of your trade.

2. *Avoid options on stocks that trade fewer than 1 million shares per day.*
   - Options are much less liquid than stocks, so we can increase our chances of getting a decent fill, and of a reliable exit, if we trade options only on the most liquid of stocks.

3. *Avoid options with spreads larger than 10 percent (e.g., 0.2 on 2.00 option).*
   - The spread is the difference between the asking price and the bid price; it is a premium you have

to pay to the exchange's market makers in order to put on the trade.

- The greater the spread, the more the underlying stock has to move to get you to a break-even point; the more the stock has to move, the greater your risk in the trade.
- A rule of thumb I like to follow is this: if a spread is greater than 0.10, I usually enter a limit order between the spread; if the spread is greater than 0.30, I usually avoid trading that option. Yes, I miss out on some great trades doing this, but that's just me. I hate to pay premium for anything (just ask my wife!).
- Some options that are heavily traded (such as options on the QQQQ) have spreads as narrow as 0.05. New rules have recently come into effect that allow options exchanges to offer spreads in 0.01 increments. This should serve options traders well, as they will then have greater pricing control, and thus narrower spreads.

4. *On short-term plays (less than two weeks), buy the next month's strike (paying attention to rule #1).*
   - For example, if today is July 6 and I want to buy EBAY calls because I think EBAY is likely to go up in price within the next one to two weeks, I would not buy the July options, since we are less than one month from July's expiration date, but would instead buy the next month out.

5. *On longer-term plays (more than two weeks), buy the strike at least two months out.*

- For example, if today is July 6 and I want to buy EBAY calls because I think EBAY is likely to go up in price within the next three to four weeks, I would not buy the next month out, since four weeks would put us in the worst phase of those options' time value decay curve. Instead, I would buy the next expiration out after that, which for EBAY means the October calls.

6. *Buy the closest in-the-money or at-the-money strike.*
   - For example, if GE is trading at 27.00, you would buy the 27.50 strike (puts or calls), but if GE is trading at 26.00, you would buy the 25.00 strike (puts or calls).
   - *Note:* In general (assuming you trade a winning system) . . .
   - Trading far OTM options have a lower winning percentage but a higher-percentage return if the trade is successful (lower premiums paid but a bigger move in the stock is needed to make a profit).
   - Trading far ITM options have a higher winning percentage but lower-percentage returns (higher premiums paid but a smaller move in the stock is needed to make a profit).

7. *If you are only trading options, commit no more than 50 percent of your total account at any one time (keep at least 50 percent reserve in cash), and spread this out over at least five positions (roughly 10 percent of your total account per trade).*

- Options are high risk. Anything less than this kind of allotment runs the risk of wiping out a significant portion of your account, and your overall returns will suffer, if you are not forced to close your account altogether. It will happen. Even with the most robust of systems, losses happen. And with options, this can mean a total loss if you are not careful to pay attention to position sizing.
- If you trade stocks and options together, as I do, I suggest putting only 20 percent of your total account into options and the remaining 80 percent of your capital to work in stocks.

8. *Be quicker to take profits on options than on stocks (because of time value decay).*
   - Losses can be held a bit longer since delta works in your favor (delta slows down as the option moves further OTM).
   - Keep in mind that even a nice gain in an option trade can disappear quickly if you hold on too long, even if the stock does not move unfavorably.
   - At all times, respect the inevitability of time value decay!

9. *Determine a percentage stop price (25 to 40 percent recommended) and set an audible alert near this price (or set an alert on the underlying stock).*
   - Do not set an actual stop-loss on options; due to their wider spread and lowered liquidity, a real

stop-loss on an option trade is not recommended.

10. *Set a limit sell order at your target based on an estimated move in the underlying × delta.*

   For example, say KLAC is trading in early July around $50 and you expect the stock to move to 55:
   - So you buy KLAC Sept 50 calls @ 5.00 (delta 0.50).
   - As soon as you are executed, you should set a limit sell order, good till canceled (GTC), at 7.50 ($5 move × 0.50; 50 percent gain).

11. *Never take more than a −40 percent loss on any options position or −5 percent of your total account, whichever is smaller.*
   - This rule holds only for the single positions, not the compound positions, which require the use of more than one option at once. In the compound positions, your potential loss is generally limited and is usually nowhere near −40 percent.
   - A 5 percent loss guarantees that you will be able to put on at least 20 options trades before you run out of money. If you can't turn a decent profit with 20 options trades, then you should be out of the game altogether.

12. *Once an option position has a profit of 50 percent, close the position if it trades down to breakeven.*
   - There is an old adage said about options: *Profits once lost rarely return.* If you have a decent return

in your options position and it suddenly fizzles back to your entry price, it is probably a good idea to close the position at breakeven to avoid a loss. Due to a variety of pricing factors, and unlike the tragic Sisyphus, options have a harder time climbing the hill the second time around.

13. *Hold all compound option positions (covered calls, bull and bear spreads) to expiration.*
    - The one exception to this rule is for the *straddle*, which you will learn about in Chapter 13.

14. *If you are profitable in a single option position (calls, puts, naked calls and puts), close the position two weeks before expiration and, if you want to remain in the position, buy the next month's position at the nearest ITM strike.*
    - This is called *rolling over* your position; if you reinvest your profits by buying a larger position in the new option, you are *pyramiding* your position. Both are good ideas as long as your position is nicely profitable. This is how you can get ten-baggers and more from options.

Okay, those are my must-follow rules for swing trading stock options. Remember, if you are going to buy or write a stock options contract, you must have a reasonable degree of confidence in the future direction of the underlying stock, just as you would if you were to buy or sell short the stock itself. For this you need a sound trading strategy. And if you employ a market-neutral approach to an options position, you need to be reasonably sure that the stock is about to make a sizeable move, one way or the other. For this, again, you need a sound trading strategy.

One final note, and it is an important one: you can be a successful stock options trader *only* if you are already a successful stock trader. It is strongly recommended that you *not* trade options until you have a proven track record of strong stock-trading gains. You can go a long time losing at the stock-trading game and still maintain enough capital to mount a comeback once you've gained the necessary experience. However, the highly leveraged nature of options ensures that losing at the stock options game is a short-lived experience.

OPTIONS STRATEGIES:
BULLISH TRENDS

IT bears repeating that you need to know, before you enter any options position, whether you are bullish, bearish, or neutral on the underlying stock, and to what degree you are so. Options trading also requires you to assess your risk tolerance so that you can select the appropriate option combination to either increase or reduce your risk exposure.

With this in mind, the following list of options-trading strategies is offered for your consideration. The list is set up to allow you to choose the best options strategy based on:

- Your directional bias on the underlying stock
- Your risk tolerance for the particular trade

Directional bias here means in which direction you see the stock moving as it trades into the near future. And *risk tolerance* refers to your confidence level regarding the trade: if it is high, you might want to assume unlimited risk (with unlimited upside potential) and use a stop-loss; if it is not very high, you might want to assume limited risk (which usually goes along with limited upside potential). Once you have decided these two elements, you are ready to select the appropriate options-trading strategy for the stock you wish to profit from.

So the first question to ask yourself is: "What is my outlook on the stock I want to trade?"

- *Bullish:* I expect a significant price rise.
- *Bearish:* I expect a significant price fall.
- *Neutral:* I expect a move up or down but am not sure which.
- *Volatile:* I expect a strong move up or down.

BULLISH STRATEGIES

Let's assume you are bullish on your stock. You have now satisfied your directional bias question. Next thing you need to do is determine your risk tolerance, or more precisely, how confident you are that your stock is going up by a significant amount.

So you now need to ask yourself, "Just how bullish am I on this stock?"

- *Very bullish:* Requires a higher-risk strategy.
- *Moderately bullish:* Requires a more conservative strategy.

Now it is time to lay out our strategies for these various scenarios.

VERY BULLISH

Strategy 1: Buy Calls

Strategy rationale: The investor thinks that the stock will rise significantly in the short term.

Strategy implementation: Call options are bought at the nearest ITM strike price.

Upside potential: The profit potential is unlimited and rises as the stock price rises.

Break-even point at expiry: Strike price plus the spread and commission.

Downside risk: Limited to the premium paid-incurred if the stock at expiry is at, or below, the strike price.

Margin: Not required.

Comment: If the market does little, then the value of the position will decrease as the option time value falls.

Strategy 2: Sell Naked Put

Strategy rationale: The investor is bullish on the stock and quite certain the stock will not decline over time.

Strategy implementation: Put options are sold or written at the nearest ATM or ITM strike without also holding a short position in the stock (hence, a *naked* put). If an investor is very bullish, then deeper ITM puts would be sold or written.

Upside potential: Profit potential is limited to the premium received. The more the option is ITM at purchase, the greater the premium received.

Break-even point at expiry: Strike price less the spread.

Downside risk: Loss is almost unlimited ("almost," since the underlying price cannot fall below zero). This is a high-risk strategy, although stops can be used to limit that risk. There is the potential for a catastrophic loss if the stock crashes overnight due to bad news.

Margin: Always required.

Comment: If the stock does little, and time passes, the position is likely to become profitable as time value in the option erodes.

MODERATELY BULLISH

Strategy 1: Bull Call or Put Spread

Strategy rationale: The investor thinks that the stock price will rise modestly and not fall, but wants to limit the downside risk just in case.

Strategy implementation: A call option is bought at the nearest ITM strike price, and another call option is sold or written at the nearest OTM strike price; this produces a debit to the account.

OR

A put option is bought at the nearest ITM strike
price, and another put option is sold or written
at the nearest OTM strike price; this produces
a credit to the account.

Upside potential (in the case of a bull call spread):
Limited to the difference between the two
strikes (normally $500 per contract) less the
initial debit; maximum profit is gained if the
stock at expiry is above the higher strike.

OR

(In the case of a bull put spread): Limited to the
initial credit; maximum profit is gained if the
stock at expiry is above the higher strike.

Downside risk (in the case of a bull call spread):
Limited only to the net initial debit; maximum
loss is seen if at expiry the stock price is below
the lower strike.

OR

(In the case of a bull put spread): Limited only to
the difference between the two strikes less
the initial credit; maximum loss is seen if at
expiry the stock price is below the lower
strike.

Margin: Required only on the calls sold or written.

Comment: Time value erosion is not too significant a

factor in this strategy due to the balanced position.

Strategy 2: Covered Calls

Strategy rationale: The investor thinks that the stock price will rise modestly over time but is worried about a possible drawdown first and wants to limit the downside risk.

Strategy implementation: The investor buys the underlying stock (hence, *covered call* as opposed to *naked call* where one does not own the stock) and sells or writes a call (1 per 100 shares owned) against the stock at the nearest OTM strike price.

Upside potential: Limited to the difference between the purchase price of the stock and the strike price, plus the credit for the call sold.

Downside risk: Limited to the drop of the underlying stock less the credit for the call sold.

Margin: Required only on the calls or puts sold or written.

Comment: Time value erosion works in your favor in this trade.

OPTIONS STRATEGIES:
BEARISH TRENDS

Now, let's assume that you are bearish on the stock you wish to purchase options on. Again, you have now satisfied your directional bias question. The next thing you need to do is determine your risk tolerance, or, more precisely, how confident you are that your stock is going down by a significant amount.

So you now need to ask yourself, "Just how bearish am I on this stock?"

- *Very bearish:* Requires a higher-risk strategy.
- *Moderately bearish:* Requires a more conservative strategy.

Now it is time to lay out our strategies for these various scenarios.

VERY BEARISH

Strategy 1: Buy Put

Strategy rationale: The investor thinks that the stock will drop significantly in the short term.

Strategy implementation: Put options are bought at the nearest ITM strike price.

Upside potential: Profit potential is unlimited and rises as the stock price declines.

Break-even point at expiry: Strike price plus the spread.

Downside risk: Limited to the premium paid— incurred if the market at expiry is at, or above, the strike price.

Margin: Not required.

Comment: If the stock does little, then the value of the position will decrease as the option time value falls.

Strategy 2: Sell Naked Call

Strategy rationale: The investor is bearish on the stock and quite certain the stock will not appreciate over time.

Strategy implementation: Call options are sold or written at the nearest ATM or ITM strike without also holding a long position in the stock (hence, a *naked* call). If an investor is very bearish on the stock, then deeper ITM calls could be sold or written.

Upside potential: Profit potential is limited to the premium received. The more the option is ITM at purchase, the greater the premium received.

Break-even point at expiry: Strike price less the spread.

Downside risk: Loss is unlimited (since in theory the price of a stock could rise to infinity). This is a high-risk strategy, although certainly stops can be used to limit that risk. There is the potential for a catastrophic loss if the stock gaps up overnight due to unexpected good news.

Margin: Always required.

Comment: If the stock does little, and time passes, the position is likely to become profitable as time value in the option erodes.

MODERATELY BEARISH

Strategy 1: Bear Call or Put Spread

Strategy rationale: The investor thinks that the stock price will rise modestly and not fall but wants to limit the downside risk just in case.

Strategy implementation: A call option is sold or written at the nearest ITM strike price, and another call option is bought at the nearest

OTM strike price; this produces a net credit to the account.

OR

A put option is sold or written at the nearest ITM strike price, and another put option is bought at the nearest OTM strike price; this produces a net debit to the account.

Upside potential (in the case of a bear call spread): Limited to the initial net credit; maximum profit is gained if the stock at expiry is below the lower strike.

OR

(In the case of a bear put spread): Limited to the difference between the two strikes (usually $500 per contract) minus the initial net debit; maximum profit is gained if the stock at expiry is above the higher strike.

Downside risk (in the case of a bear call spread): Limited only to the difference between the two strikes minus the initial net credit; maximum loss is seen if at expiry the stock price is above the higher strike.

OR

(In the case of a bear put spread): Limited only to the net initial debit; maximum loss is seen if at

expiry the stock price is above the higher
strike.

Margin: Required only on the calls or puts sold or
written.

Comment: Time value erosion is not too significant a
factor in this strategy due to the balanced
position.

OPTIONS STRATEGIES: NEUTRAL

THE EARNINGS SEASON PLAY

In this section, I am going to introduce you to one of my favorite options strategies, which can be used only at certain times of the year: the four *earnings seasons*. The timing of earnings seasons will vary slightly from year to year as different companies change their earnings dates over time. For the most part, they follow the changes of the seasons. Generally, whenever a new season begins—winter, spring, summer, fall—we can look forward to a fresh batch of earnings reports over the next four to five weeks.

With earnings reports comes a well-recognized phenomenon: incredible market volatility. The options strategy I will outline in this chapter—called the *straddle*, one of the most mechanical of all options-trading strategies—will show you how to capitalize on this volatility.

In its simplest form—straddle on, straddle off—we can expect returns from a straddle position in the +10 to +20 percent range for a hold that can last anywhere from two to five days. As long as you follow my rules to the letter as listed here, you should expect about a 60 percent win rate with this strategy. And because this is a compound position (i.e., both long and short at the same time), the losses when incurred are normally small. In its more complex form—leg into the straddle, leg out of the straddle—returns can run to +50 percent or more in five to eight trading days (*legging in* and *legging out* will be defined later). Both the simple and the complex forms are taught here. I will first narrate the trading strategy, then I will offer a more concise summary at the end of this chapter.

FINDING THE RIGHT STOCKS

What we are looking for when we put a straddle on a stock during earnings season is an optionable, liquid, highly volatile stock that is just about to report to the public its quarterly earnings results, and which at past earnings reports has fluctuated wildly in price. Whether the stock tends to trade up or down following earnings does not matter; what matters is that it tends to move big one way or the other. Three days before the report goes public, we are going to put on (the simple version), or leg into (the complex version), what is called a *straddle*. We will hold this position for up to five days following the announcement (up to seven days in all), during which time we will look to take the position off, in most cases, for a nice profit.

First, let's go over the search process step by step. A successful straddle play requires a stock that satisfies the following six criteria:

1. It is going to report its earnings three market days from now.

2. It is going to report its earnings after the market close, on Monday through Thursday (normally no company reports earnings on a Friday).

3. It is a volatile or high-beta stock.

4. It is a liquid stock (it has a large daily volume).

5. It is priced over $40 (the higher, the better).

6. It has a history of gapping up or down more than $1.00 on the day after its earnings announcement.

The first step is to find a stock that is about to report earnings. This is easily done with a free search of Yahoo! Finance's earnings calendar. You will find a link for this calendar at http://biz.yahoo.com/r/. Look under "Company Earnings" for the Earnings Dates link. Click on that link and you will come to a page that lists, day by day, all the companies that are reporting earnings for the current week. You can also click ahead to the next week to see what is coming up. When you do that, you should be looking at a page that looks something like Table 15.1.

Alcoa is the company thought to usher in each new earnings season, since it is listed first in any alphabetically ordered list and thus is given a privileged position among the companies announcing their earnings (one of those funny Wall Street rituals). So once AA reports, it is time to begin scanning the earnings announcement pages like the one shown in Table 15.1. Early in the season you will see about this number of companies reporting each day, 10 to 20. But the pace quickly picks up, and during the thick

TABLE 15.1   Earnings Announcement Schedule from Yahoo!

Brown & Brown	BRO	0.45	After Market Close	Add	
Cintas Corporation	CTAS	0.41	After Market Close	Add	Listen
Electronics for Imaging	EFII	0.24	Time Not Supplied	Add	
GenCorp Inc.	GY	N/A	Before Market Open	Add	Listen
Helen of Troy Ltd	HELE	0.45	Before Market Open	Add	Listen
Horizon Health Corporation	HORC	0.47	After Market Close	Add	Listen
M&T Bank Corporation	MTB	1.45	Before Market Open	Add	
M.D.C Holdings	MDC	1.93	After Market Close	Add	
Micrologix Biotech	MBI.TO	N/A	Time Not Supplied	Add	
Novellus Systems, Inc.	NVLS	0.26	Time Not Supplied	Add	
Orckit Communications	ORCT	N/A	Time Not Supplied	Add	
Pace Micro Technology plc	PIC.L	N/A	Before Market Open	Add	
Stanley Furniture	STLY	0.68	After Market Close	Add	
Summit Bankshares	SBIT	0.42	After Market Close	Add	
SunTrust	STI	1.26	Before Market Open	Add	
Universal Forest Products, Inc.	UFPI	1.04	After Market Close	Add	Listen

of the season you will see numbers well over 100 reporting each day. When we are out of earnings season, you may see several days without any companies reporting.

We want a stock that is going to report in three trading days. Assume that today is July 19. I will therefore be looking for a stock that is set to report on July 22 after the close. The reason we look only at those stocks that report after the market closes is that the larger moves occur then, as the news has a chance to be reported overnight to a larger audience. It allows both evening traders and morning traders to have a chance to move the shares.

Here is part of the actual list of companies that were set to publicly report their earnings on July 22, 2006. As you can see from this partial list (only A through C companies), we are now in the thick of the earnings season (Table 15.2).

This is a long list (and we are only up to the C's), but we can soon whittle it down to a manageable number. First, we eliminate all those stocks that report "before market open." We are not interested in those. We can also delete those where "time [is] not supplied." Most of those are smaller companies we wouldn't want to trade in any case. So, after the first round of elimination, this is what we are left with:

ARDI	BHL	CPKI	PWN	CBU
ADVS	BORL	ELY	CATT	CPSI
AMZN	BFAM	CBM	CLS	CPWR
ARTG	BDN	CMO	COBZ	CR
ABTL	BRCM	CPTV	COHU	CYT

Of the list that remains, we want to select only those companies that trade at least 1 million shares each day and are reasonably volatile (they trade up and down wildly at a pace quicker than either the Nasdaq or the S&P 500). If you are an active trader, as I am, and you work from a watch list of stocks selected for their high volume and volatility, as I do, you only need eyeball the preceding list to recognize your favorite high-beta stocks to short-list. But if you are not familiar with the symbols of the most

TABLE 15.2   Earnings Announcement Schedule: Mid-Season

@Road	ARDI	0.06	After Market Close	Add	
Abitibi-Consolidated	ABY	N/A	Time Not Supplied	Add	
Adolph Coors, Co.	RKY	1.99	Before Market Open	Add	
Advanced Power Technology, Inc.	APTI	0.10	4:15 pm ET	Add	Listen
Advent Software	ADVS	0.02	After Market Close	Add	Listen
Alaska Airlines	ALK	−0.06	Before Market Open	Add	Listen
Albemarle Corporation	ALB	0.42	Time Not Supplied	Add	Listen
Alberto-Culver Co.	ACV	0.54	Time Not Supplied	Add	Listen
Align Technology	ALGN	0.06	Before Market Open	Add	Listen
Alliance Resource Partners LP	ARLP	0.93	Time Not Supplied	Add	
Alltel Corp.	AT	0.81	Time Not Supplied	Add	
Amazon.com, Inc.	AMZN	0.19	After Market Close	Add	Listen
Ambassadors International, Inc.	AMIE	0.04	Before Market Open	Add	Listen
American Axle & Manufacturing Holdings	AXL	1.03	Time Not Supplied	Add	
American International Group	AIG	1.12	Before Market Open	Add	
American Pharmaceutical Partners, Inc.	APPX	0.16	Time Not Supplied	Add	
AmeriSourceBergen	ABC	0.98	Before Market Open	Add	Listen
Amgen	AMGN	0.59	Time Not Supplied	Add	Listen
Aptimus	APTM.OB	N/A	Time Not Supplied	Add	
Arbitron Inc.	ARB	0.27	Before Market Open	Add	Listen
Art Technology Group	ARTG	N/A	After Market Close	Add	Listen
Artesyn Technologies, Inc	ATSN	0.06	Before Market Open	Add	

Astoria Financial Corporation	AF	0.79	Before Market Open	Add	Listen
Astral Media Inc	ACMa.TO	N/A	Time Not Supplied	Add	
AstraZeneca PLC	AZN	0.48	Time Not Supplied	Add	
Astronics	ATRO	N/A	Before Market Open	Add	
AT&T	T	0.08	Before Market Open	Add	Listen
Atherogenics, Inc.	AGIX	−0.45	Before Market Open	Add	
Autobytel.com	ABTL	0.03	After Market Close	Add	
Autoliv	ALV	0.88	06:00 am ET	Add	
Avici Systems, Inc.	AVCI	−0.63	Time Not Supplied	Add	Listen
Avocent Corporation	AVCT	0.30	Time Not Supplied	Add	Listen
Axfood AB	AXFO.ST	N/A	Time Not Supplied	Add	
Becton, Dickinson and Company	BDX	0.64	Before Market Open	Add	Listen
Bemis Company, Inc.	BMS	0.42	Before Market Open	Add	Listen
Benchmark Electronics	BHE	0.37	Before Market Open	Add	
Bennett Environmental	BEL	0.04	Time Not Supplied	Add	Listen
Berkshire Hills Bancorp	BHL	0.44	After Market Close	Add	
Black & Decker Corporation	BDK	1.26	Before Market Open	Add	
Borland Software Corporation	BORL	0.06	After Market Close	Add	
Boston Private Financial Holdings	BPFH	0.29	Time Not Supplied	Add	
Brandywine Realty Trust	BDN	0.63	Time Not Supplied	Add	Listen
Bright Horizons Family Solutions	BFAM	0.47	After Market Close	Add	Listen
Broadcom	BRCM	0.32	After Market Close	Add	Listen
Caesars Entertainment	CZR	0.17	Before Market Open	Add	Listen
California Pizza Kitchen	CPKI	0.25	After Market Close	Add	

TABLE 15.2   Earnings Announcement Schedule:
Mid-Season (Continued)

Callaway Golf	ELY	0.22	After Market Close	Add	
Cambrex	CBM	0.26	After Market Close	Add	
Capita Group	CPI.L	N/A	Time Not Supplied	Add	
Capital City Bank Group	CCBG	0.48	Before Market Open	Add	
Capstead Mortgage Corporation	CMO	N/A	After Market Close	Add	
Captiva Software Corp.	CPTV	0.09	After Market Close	Add	
Cash America International	PWN	0.24	After Market Close	Add	
Catapult Communications	CATT	0.17	After Market Close	Add	Listen
Caterpillar Inc.	CAT	1.71	Before Market Open	Add	Listen
CDI Corp.	CDI	0.30	Before Market Open	Add	
Celestica	CLS	0.09	After Market Close	Add	
CenterPoint Energy	CNP	0.19	Before Market Open	Add	Listen
Ceragon Networks Ltd	CRNT	0.01	Before Market Open	Add	
Certegy	CEY	0.38	Before Market Open	Add	
Chartered Semiconductor Manufacturing	CHRT	0.05	Time Not Supplied	Add	
Chicago Mercantile Hldgs Inc	CME	1.66	Before Market Open	Add	Listen
Chittenden	CHZ	0.51	Before Market Open	Add	Listen
Chordiant Software	CHRD	0.02	Time Not Supplied	Add	
Cincinnati Financial Corporation	CINF	0.59	Before Market Open	Add	
Circor International	CIR	0.27	Time Not Supplied	Add	
CIT Group	CIT	0.80	Before Market Open	Add	
CNS, Inc.	CNXS	0.11	Time Not Supplied	Add	Listen
CoBiz Inc.	COBZ	0.16	After Market Close	Add	
Cohu	COHU	0.19	After Market Close	Add	

CollaGenex Pharmaceuticals, Inc.	CGPI	0.24	Before Market Open	Add
Commercial Federal Corp.	CFB	0.47	Before Market Open	Add Listen
Community Bancorp Inc.	CMBC	0.42	Time Not Supplied	Add
Community Bank System	CBU	0.39	After Market Close	Add Listen
Compania de Minas Buenaventura	BVN	0.38	Time Not Supplied	Add
Computer Access Technology Corporation	CATZ	0.02	08:30 am ET	Add Listen
Computer Associates International	CA	0.18	Time Not Supplied	Add
Computer Programs and Systems, Inc.	CPSI	0.14	After Market Close	Add Listen
Compuware Corporation	CPWR	0.03	After Market Close	Add Listen
CONMED	CNMD	0.41	Before Market Open	Add Listen
Consolidated Edison, Inc.	ED	0.26	Time Not Supplied	Add
Cooper Industries Ltd.	CBE	0.86	Before Market Open	Add
Cooper Tire & Rubber	CTB	0.39	Time Not Supplied	Add Listen
Corus Entertainment Inc.	CJRb.TO	N/A	5:00 pm ET	Add
CorVel	CRVL	0.32	Time Not Supplied	Add
Countrywide Financial Corporation	CFC	2.26	08:00 am ET	Add Listen
Crane	CR	0.51	After Market Close	Add
Curon Medical, Inc.	CURN	−0.15	Time Not Supplied	Add
Cytec Industries Inc.	CYT	0.72	After Market Close	Add Listen

volatile stocks (and, hence, the best trend-trading stocks), then we have provided here for you an easy method for checking.

To check for average daily volume and volatility, simply type the stock ticker at the end of this URL (after the "=" sign) and paste it into your Web browser. Once it is in your browser, simply delete the symbol and type in another one to check the full list:

http://finance.yahoo.com/q/ks?s=

This is the Key Statistics page from Yahoo! Finance, which will give you a reading both of the average daily volume and of beta, which, as mentioned, is a function of the stock's volatility relative to the S&P 500. Here, then, are the rules for further elimination using this information:

- Eliminate all stocks with less than 1 million daily shares traded.
- Eliminate all stocks with less than 2.0 beta.
- Eliminate all stocks priced less than 40.00.

This process of elimination has now whittled our list of A—C stocks down to two: AMZN and BRCM. No surprises there. To all active traders—at least at this writing—these are very familiar symbols, and are nearly always on the list of great trading vehicles.

The next thing we do with these two stocks is go to the charts and ask this question: What have AMZN and BRCM done in the previous two quarters at the announce-

ment of earnings—are they overbought, oversold, or somewhere in between?

AMZN last reported earnings after the bell on April
22. In anticipation of the announcement, traders ran price
up to a short-term high, and they were right: the news was
great. AMZN beat estimates by +21 percent! However, on
the day following the announcement, the market sold off
strongly overnight on the news (it's another one of those
weird Wall Street rituals!), and the stock gapped down.
This signaled a buying opportunity to traders, who then
rallied the stock back up into resistance (see Figure 15.1).

That is exactly the kind of volatility that can turn a
straddle into an easy winner. This is just what we are looking for when we go back to the previous two quarters'
announcements.

Two quarters ago, AMZN again showed great move-

Figure 15.1   AMZN showing earnings volatility.

ment. The stock was overbought and near new 52-week highs. Earnings came in cold, and the stock gapped down sharply and then went into a tailspin for several weeks. Figure 15.2 is what the chart looked like.

Again, another easy winner for the straddle strategy. Clearly, AMZN is going on our list of straddles to put on. It satisfies all our criteria: it is optionable and highly liquid, it has a high beta (is very volatile), and it goes absolutely bonkers at earnings time.

Now, let's take a quick look at BRCM. Like AMZN, BRCM reported after the bell on April 22, 2004. In anticipation, traders took a greatly oversold stock and ran it up strongly (this is perfect for our legging-in strategy—see later description). On the day of earnings, BRCM gapped up strongly to continue the trend, then the shares met with resistance. It came crashing back down again over the next several days (see Figure 15.3).

Figure 15.2   AMZN showing earnings volatility.

Figure 15.3   BRCM showing earnings volatility.

In the previous quarter, BRCM did something very similar. It ran up into the earnings announcement, gapped up hugely the day after the announcement was made, then proceeded to sell off for several days after that (see Figure 15.4).

Now we will add both AMZN and BRCM to our list of straddles to put on. They have satisfied all our entry requirements, and both are great candidates for huge returns during the week of July 19, as we straddle each stock with a pair of options.

The next thing we want to know is this: where are these stocks with respect to oversold or overbought levels three days before earnings are announced? If we get a clear oversold or overbought reading on that day, then we are given a green light to leg into the straddle trade. If not, then we will have to wait to put the straddle on into the close of the day that earnings are to be reported. Both

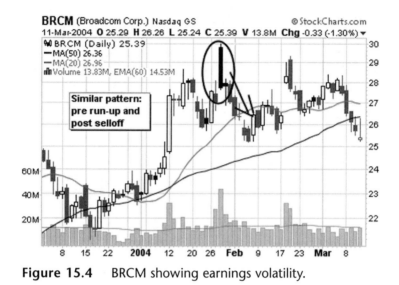

Figure 15.4   BRCM showing earnings volatility.

AMZN and BRCM, as mentioned, are announcing after the close on July 22. This means that we will check their charts on July 19 to determine these levels.

We use the following technical indicators to tell us just where these stocks are on the oversold-overbought spectrum:

- RSI (5) reading
  - *Less than 30 (oversold) or more than 70 (overbought)*
- Stochastics %K (5) reading
  - *Less than 25 (oversold) or more than 75 (overbought)*
- CCI (20) reading
  - *Less than −100 (oversold) or more than +100 (overbought)*

We need to see at least two out of three of these indicators give oversold or overbought readings in order to get a green light to leg into the trade. On July 10, BRCM had readings of 24.6, 6.24, and −140.5. AMZN had readings of 18.3, 23.17, and −108.4. Clearly, both stocks are in an oversold condition. If these numbers were to hold until July 19 (three days before each announces earnings), we would then have given the green light to leg into these straddles. Again, if we do not get a green light, we will not leg into the trade. We will wait until the day of earnings to put on both sides of the straddle.

> **Definition:** *Legging into* an options straddle occurs when we buy each side of the straddle— the calls and the puts—on different market days. *Legging out of* an options straddle occurs when we sell each side of the straddle on different market days. The alternative is simply called *putting on* the straddle: here both sides of the trade are bought on the same market day, and usually at the same time.

Legging in is the preferred mode of entry, since it has the potential of maximizing our gains. But this is a more complex form of the straddle and requires some market timing. The simpler form of the straddle is to put the straddle on during the day that earnings are to be announced. This can be done in the morning or afternoon; it doesn't matter. In both cases, however, we will be legging out of the trade. Just how these are all done will be explained later.

Keep in mind that a straddle is a market-neutral strategy, meaning that we are not sure going into the trade in which direction the stock is likely to go after we put the position on. We just believe that the stock will move, and move big, in response to its earnings announcement. Whether it moves up or down makes no difference to us. We will profit either way as long as the move is big enough.

The straddle is also, like the bull and bear spreads previously described, a *compound* trade. This means that we are going to enter and exit more than one type of option. We will, in fact, be buying both a call and a put. These may be bought at separate times, which is what we mean by *legging into* and *legging out of* the trade. Here is how we define the straddle play.

MARKET NEUTRAL

Strategy: Straddle

Strategy rationale: The investor thinks that the stock will be very volatile in the short term but does not know which way the stock will move.

Strategy implementation: The call option and the put option are bought at the same ATM strike price; if the stock price is between two strikes, then the call and the put are each bought at the nearest strike.

Upside potential: Unlimited.

Break-even point at expiry: This trade is never held to

expiration; the trade always remains at or near
breakeven less spread and time value decay
Downside risk: Limited to the two premiums paid.
Margin: Not required.
Comment: The position loses value with the passage
of time as the time value decreases on options.

PUTTING ON THE STRADDLE

Now we are ready to put the trade on. We have two options
here: either we leg into the trade, meaning that we will buy
the two sides of the position on different days, or we will
simply put the trade on by buying both sides together.

We are given a green light to leg into the trade when
the stock is either oversold or overbought three days before
the earnings announcement. Here are the rules for legging
into the trade:

Three days before earnings, check the chart.
- If oversold, buy the call options at the close of
  that day, and on the day of the earnings announcement, buy the puts at the close.
- If overbought, buy the put options at the close
  of that day, and on the day of the earnings announcement, buy the calls at the close.

That is how we leg into the trade. Of course, you can tin-
ker a bit with the "buy at the close" idea. If you are going
to leg into the calls, for example, and the market is strong
in the morning, you might want to buy them earlier in the

day rather than only at the end. But the simplest entry is to buy them just a few minutes before the market closes at 4 p.m. EST. Keep in mind that options do *not* trade in after-hours trading (at least not yet—in the future they likely will).

Legging into the straddle position is a strategy aimed at maximizing the potential return of one side of the trade prior to the big move. The theory here is that in an over-sold or overbought market, traders will move the stock in the opposite direction a few days before the announcement in anticipation of a contrary move after the announcement.

The other mode of entry is less complex. If we do not get a green light to leg into the trade, we will simply buy both sides of the trade, both call and put options, sometime before the close on the day of the announcement.

Here is an important note: we want to buy the same strike price for each side of the trade, and it should be the nearest strike possible. Choosing an expiration month will follow the same rules for all options trades as listed previously.

TAKING OFF A STRADDLE

We have selected our stocks to straddle and have entered both sides of the trade: calls and puts. Now we need to know how long to hold both. Here is how we do this.

We expect a large move to occur in the stock over-night as the numbers are announced and speculators pile on orders in the after-market trading period. By 9:30 a.m. EST, when the market opens the next day, we should see a sizeable gap in price relative to the previous day's close. If the gap is up, then our calls are going to ramp up in value and become winners for us. If the gap is down, then our puts are going to ramp up in value and become winners for us. Of course, the opposite is true for the other side of the trade. In a gap up our puts are going to stink, and in a gap down our calls are going to stink. But here is the great thing about options, and what makes the straddle such a low-risk play: because of the delta factor, the losing side of the trade will not lose as much as the winning side of the trade will win.

As mentioned previously, delta, or the rate of change in an option's premium to change in the value of the underlying stock, increases as a trade moves more and more in-the-money, and it decreases as a trade moves more and more out-of-the-money. In other words, a big gap up will increase the value of our calls more than it decreases the value of our puts—and vice versa on a gap down. To our bottom line, this means that as long as the stock moves big, we should always show a profit on the trade because of the delta factor, and normally that profit is large enough to cover commissions and the spread and still post a solid double-digit-percentage winner.

Now, after the opening gap, what usually happens is that a "fade the news" mentality takes over, and traders seek to close the gap. This is not always the case, so we always have to anticipate a run in the direction of the gap. Often, however, the gap will close and the market runs in the opposite direction (a move we call, poetically, *gap and crap*). With all this in mind, we can now establish our rules for closing out the straddle position.

Here is how we take off the straddle.

If the market was *oversold* (we legged into the straddle) and *gaps up* more than $1.00 on the open after the announcement:

- We will sell our puts at the open and hold our calls.
- We will hold our calls for every day the stock puts in a green candle (close is higher than the open) up to five trading days after the announcement.
- If we are still in our calls on the fifth trading day after the announcement, we will sell them at the close.

If the market was *oversold* (we legged into the straddle) and *gaps down* more than $1.00 on the open after the announcement:

- We will sell our calls at the open and hold our puts.
- We will hold our puts for every day the stock puts in a red candle (close is lower than the open) up to five trading days after the announcement.
- If we are still in our puts on the fifth trading day after the announcement, we will sell them at the close.

If the market was *overbought* (we legged into the straddle) and *gaps down* more than $1.00 on the open after the announcement:

- We will sell our calls at the open and hold our puts.
- We will hold our puts for every day the stock puts in a red candle (close is lower than the open) up to five trading days after the announcement.
- If we are still in our puts on the fifth trading day after the announcement, we will sell them at the close.

If the market was *overbought* (we legged into the straddle) and *gaps up* more than $1.00 on the open after the announcement:

- We will sell our puts at the open and hold our calls.
- We will hold our calls for every day the stock puts in a green candle (close is higher than the open) up to five trading days after the announcement.
- If we are still in our calls on the fifth trading day after the announcement, we will sell them at the close.

If the market was *neither oversold nor overbought* (we did not leg into the straddle) and *gaps up or down* more than $1.00 on the open after the announcement:

- We will sell the winning side of the trade (calls in a gap up, puts in a gap down) at the open and hold the losing side of the trade.

- We will hold our calls for every day the stock puts in a green candle, or puts for every day the stock puts in a red candle, up to five trading days after the announcement.
- If we are still in our calls or puts on the fifth trading day after the announcement, we will sell them at the close.

If the market fails to gap more than $1.00 at the open, then we have a judgment call to make. Generally, if the gap is between $0.50 and $1.00, we can still simply follow the rules as listed previously. The larger the dollar amount of the gap, however, the more profitable the trade will be. This is why it is so important to select stocks that are higher in price, are very volatile, and have had a history of multibucker gaps at earnings.

But if in the event a stock that has met all our other conditions fails to open with a gap larger than $0.50, here are the general rules to follow:

- If the market is *oversold*: sell the puts and hold the calls, as previously described.
- If the market is *overbought*: sell the calls and hold the puts, as previously described.
- If the market is neither *oversold* nor *overbought*: sell the losing side of the trade and hold the winning side, as previously described.

Our expected returns on any straddle depend a lot on whether we legged in or not (we will always leg out). A perfect straddle trade is one where we generate a nice profit in the three days prior to earnings on our first leg in. We have to cash it out the next day on the gap for less than our maximum profit, but we still bank, say, +10 percent. Then the other side of the trade, which we just bought on the day of earnings, gets a great ramp-up on the following day's gap (let's say it ramps up 25 percent on the close) and continues to run for the next five days. By the close of the fifth day, it may have doubled in premium value. This would give us a total return on investment of +55 percent (+110 percent total divided by 2) in eight trading days. While not all straddles run this well, enough do if you follow our rules to the letter to make this a very profitable system. Losses are normally small and usually just involve the loss of some time value and the loss on spreads and commissions.

While these returns may sound ideal, keep in mind that straddles work only during the peak of earnings season, so we have only about a 12- to 16-week window each year. Moreover, there are quiet market cycles when even the most volatile of stocks do not move that much in response to earnings. During the straddle off-season, or when the markets are less volatile, we will need to turn to one or more of the other options strategies listed in the previous two chapters.

THE STRADDLE STRATEGY: AN 11-POINT REVIEW

The straddle is one of the best trading strategies you can have in your arsenal of strategies. It takes some practice to execute correctly, however, so the best advice I can give is to trade the straddle initially with a very small amount of capital (you can start with just one contract per side to get the feel of it). But after an earnings season or two, you should be able to put straddles on and off with some degree of comfort.

Here is a review of the system as we outlined it in this chapter:

1. Get a list of stocks reporting earnings three trading days from today.

2. Eliminate all stocks not reporting earnings after the bell.

3. Eliminate all stocks not trading more than 1 million shares per day.

4. Eliminate all stocks with a beta less than 2.0.

5. Eliminate all stocks priced less than 40.00.

6. Check the chart to determine whether the stock gapped more than $1.00 at its last two earnings announcements. Eliminate those that did not.

7. Check the chart to determine whether the stock is *oversold* or *overbought* using the following indicators:
   - RSI (5) reading: *less than 30 (oversold) or more than 70 (overbought)*
   - Stochastics %K (5) reading: *less than 25 (oversold) or more than 75 (overbought)*
   - CCI (20) reading: *less than −100 (oversold) or more than +100 (overbought)*

8. We need agreement from any two of these indicators to register an *oversold* or *overbought*

condition. If we get such a condition, then we will leg into the trade:

- Buy the calls three days before earnings if oversold.
- Buy the puts three days before earnings if overbought.
- Then buy the other half of the trade before the close on the day of the earnings announcement.

9. If neither *oversold* nor *overbought*, we will buy both sides of the trade on the day of the announcement.

10. We will buy the same strike price for each side of the trade, and it will be the nearest strike possible. The expiration month chosen should follow the same rules for all options trades, as listed in Chapter 12.

11. We will hold both sides over the earnings announcement, then leg out of the trade using the rules listed in the previous section.

There is no substitute for hard work and real-time, real-money experience when it comes to mastering the fine art of trend-trading options. You have in this and the preceding two chapters a number of strategies for enhancing your trend-trading returns using stock options. Now is the time to put this information to work. Start small: buy a couple of calls or puts instead of shares in a stock that meets one of our trend-trading setups. After you are comfortable with that, try one of the compound strategies listed here. If we are in earnings season, try the straddle. You may soon find yourself preferring options to stocks. But let me repeat a warning I stated at the beginning of this section on options: don't even think about trend-trading options until you are first a profitable trader of stocks. The leverage found in options, along with the various factors that weigh against your profit margin (the spread, time value decay, decreasing delta), will soon bring your trading career to a swift demise if you haven't yet mastered the art of trend trading.

PART
FIVE

TRADING FOR
A LIVING

THE BIGGER VISION: WHERE TREND TRADING CAN TAKE YOU

IN this last chapter of the book, I'd like to share with you two things. First, I want to talk about some of the life lessons that can be learned from trading. I'm of the opinion that if you are not willing to learn these lessons, if pride prevents you from building the kind of character that can both trade well and live well at the same time, then you are much better off—and your friends and family are much better off—if you can find some other way to improve your income.

And second, I want to share with you a vision I have for where I'd like to see the whole stock-trading phenomenon go over the next decade or two. It is a vision born out of both my love for the trading game and my sense that it can provide immense benefit to a large, growing, and increasingly frustrated demographic in our society: the overworked, underpaid, and, all too often, exploited worker.

TRADE FOR A LIVING; TRADE FOR LIFE

The phrase that begins this section is the motto I gave to Befriendthetrend.com at its inception back in October of

2002. The first half of the motto is taken from the title of Alexander Elder's famous book, the book that so greatly influenced my shift from fundamental to technical analysis (read the story in the Introduction) and, of course, that so greatly influenced the title of this book. I have always loved the phrase *trading for a living*. It evokes all the hope and promise that caused so many doctors and lawyers back in the late 1990s to leave their lucrative jobs and set up trading stations in the basements of their suburban homes, and so many busboys and taxi drivers to buy shares of Amazon and Qualcomm in between shifts. To trade is to hope: to hope for a better life. But unlike many other hope-inducing schemes, trading is one that can reasonably fulfill what it promises.

I am convinced that anyone with the right mindset, strategic tools, and real-time experience can become a successful trader—successful enough to get out of debt, pay cash for a daughter's college education, retire early, and endow a scholarship at an alma mater.

Beyond financial success, however, the school of trading can also be an important teacher of character. This is where the second half of our motto comes in: not only can trading provide a good living, it can also help you "get a life." Traders sometimes get a bad rap for being self-centered egomaniacs, and no doubt this is true for some of the better-known names in the business. In many ways Wall Street functions a lot like Las Vegas: the enticement of a huge payoff has a tendency to lure some of humanity's most seriously flawed characters. However, for every "mad money" clown, there are 10 serious, principled, self-possessed traders grunting out a solid living for themselves and their families with great integrity and generosity of spirit. I'm convinced that they are that way, at least in part, *because of* their trading. Funny thing about trading: it has this odd way of reinforcing virtuous habits of character.

Let me suggest five ways in which trading can help you improve your presence in this world. Is your spouse anxious now that you are thinking about taking up trading for a living? Then hand him or her this part of the book. Spouses might be surprised to learn that the people they are married to may well become better spouses as a result of their trading careers.

Trading Teaches Patience

Probably the most obvious lesson you can learn from trading is to be more patient. Whether you are planning to hold a trade for several weeks or only a few minutes, successful trading requires patience. Patience means the good-natured willingness to *suffer* (the Latin root of the word *patience* means "to suffer") from the delay of an anticipated good. In trading, the good anticipated is a healthy profit. Oftentimes market conditions are such that that good is delayed or even negated altogether. What do impatient traders do? They act impulsively; they panic; they make mistakes. They trade in and out when they should be holding. They dump small losers just before they turn into winners, and they dump small winners just before they turn into jackpots. No, impatient, impulsive traders will never win at the trading game. Then who wins? Those with the *fortitude*—a cardinal virtue, by the way, according to St. Thomas Aquinas—to wait out the markets day in and day out as they patiently apply their time-tested trend-trading systems.

In addition to trading, I am also a runner. I've run one marathon (and will *never* do that again!) and dozens of 5K and 10K races, and I put in 20 to 30 miles per week on the roads around our home. Running is a great deal like trading. On a long training run, it is imperative that you settle into a quiet, efficient pace in order to put in the miles needed to build up the capacity to endure the faster pace of the race. Go out too quickly and you risk breaking down before your goal distance. The correct pacing on a long run requires patience: the runner must hold himself back, not impulsively surge forward, in order to complete the goal. The same is true with trading. The trading game is a marathon run, not a sprint, and to win it you must patiently pace yourself.

Trading Teaches You How to Listen

To read a chart properly, you have to pay close attention to what the chart is trying to say. You have to develop the skill of listening to something other than yourself. Too many of us today are great at tuning in to ourselves. We engage for blissful hours in self-dialogue, and when speaking with others we are constantly thinking of ways to turn the conversation back to what we really want to talk about. Few of us are very good at listening. Do you want to be a great trader? Then you must become a great listener.

The chart is a pictorial form of language. The price patterns, the indicators, the ebb and flow of volume: these are the words charts use to speak to us. The trader must be able to hear what is said and respond appropriately. Sometimes charts just speak noise. We avoid those charts. Sometimes charts speak beautiful music. Those are the charts we play. In either case, we need to listen attentively to hear what the charts have to say.

Listen to this, men: according to all the polls, what do women want most in a man? No, not *that*! What women want most is a man who will listen to them, pay attention to them, a man who will "get" them. Guys, write this down: trading can make you a better listener, and that can make you downright sexy!

Trading Teaches You How to Be Forgiving

Imagine this scenario: you run your scans, you eyeball your charts, and after several hours of intensive research you come up with what looks to be the best trade of the week. In fact, this chart is the best-looking chart you have seen in a long time. The markets have been choppy and tough to trade lately, but this setup looks like a surefire winner. So at the open you fire off your stop-limit order to enter the trade, and sure enough, half an hour later it executes. You are now long XYZ in size. It closes the first day with a +3 percent profit—not a bad start. It closes the second day at a +5 percent profit, and the third day at +7 percent. All is well, and you envision the trade hitting your +15 percent profit target by the end of next week. That evening, however, the company comes out with some bad news: earnings are not going to be as great as everyone expected and so the company is lowering its guidance figures by a considerable amount. The next day, the stock opens below your entry price and proceeds very quickly to trade down through your stop-loss. You are out of the trade with a loss. In a quick Wall Street minute your hopes have been dashed.

How do you feel at this point? I'll tell you how you feel. You feel betrayed and resentful. The company's management let you down. They are bumbling idiots. It's all their fault! Or, if you are a neurotic like me, you will blame yourself. You should have done more research. You should have taken some profits while you had the chance. You should have seen that internal weakness in the chart. If only this, and if only that, you will say. Regret and shame color your mood.

Now, those are perfectly understandable emotional responses to a disappointing experience. But are they the best way to respond to a trade gone bad? Of course not. Over time, those negative experiences (and at times they will come in large batches) will eventually drive you out of the trading game if you can't get a handle on them. This is precisely what trading teaches us to do: in order to get beyond the blame game or the "woe is me" game, we need to learn the art of forgiveness. Forgive the company for mishandling a bad quarter. Forgive the chart for not drawing your attention more strongly to that hidden pocket of weakness. Forgive yourself for not being diligent enough, or prescient enough, or *whatever* enough. Forgive and forget and move on to the next trade. It is an essential lesson to learn in life—to forgive the mistakes of others as well as your own—and it is an essential lesson to learn in the process of trading for life.

Trading Teaches You to Hold Your Biases Loosely

A bias is simply a partiality I hold toward some expected outcome. Negatively, biases can hinder us from evaluating a situation objectively. Positively, a bias is often the only reason I would evaluate a situation in the first place. Let me illustrate. It is often said that there is a liberal bias in the media today. For the sake of argument, let's assume that that is true. Negatively, this means that media investigations of an event may not provide us with an objective reading of what actually happened. Instead, what we get is an assessment from the liberal perspective, not the whole story. But positively, that liberal bias is likely what initiated the investigation in the first place. Without that bias, there might not have been enough interest to generate a news story at all. Hence, biases can play a productive role if kept in check: they generate the initial interest in an outcome and give that outcome its significance.

Statistics defines accurate results as results that are free of all bias. Science defines a well-designed study as one that is free of all bias. But stock trading is not so objective. We need an initial bias—bullish, bearish, or something in between—in order to generate our initial interest in, and then our directional commitment toward, a particular trading outcome. We need a sense of where we see the markets headed over the short term at least so that we can apply the most profitable trading systems for that market type. And we need to know whether the chart we are scrutinizing is more likely to move up, down, or sideways in the near future. This is why trend traders use technical analysis: moving averages, trendlines, candlesticks, and indicators all help us build a rational, probabilistic bias toward the markets in general as well as toward our individual trades.

Traders get into trouble, however, when they cling too closely to their biases. Learn this market mantra: *"Let the markets do what they want to do!"* If our bias gets us into a trade and it turns out that our bias was wrong, we need to cling loosely enough to it to let it go. Too strong a bias will prevent us from doing what we should be doing with a trade gone bad: taking the quick loss and moving on. Biases can also hurt us with our winners. How many times have we held on to a nice winner, believing in our bias that it would be a big jackpot win only to see those paper profits dwindle to nothing? All too often, no doubt. So again, traders need to hold an initial bias toward the markets and truly commit themselves to it in the form of real-money trades, but they must also refuse to cling to that bias when it proves to be a misread.

Trading Teaches You to Be Humble

This brings us to our last lesson: along with holding loosely to our biases, trading teaches us to hold loosely to our pride. The markets are just too big for any mere mortal to conquer. There are too many vectors, too many inputs, too many inter- and intramarket relationships, for any single person to get a handle on them all—but put together a string of healthy winners and you will soon feel like you are (blast the fanfare) Master of the Market Domain! Strike down that attitude as soon as you feel it creeping up on you. No one—not Buffett, not Cramer, not Seykota, not Soros—masters the market. The best we can do is to learn time-tested systems that put as much probability on our side as possible, and then be diligent in applying those systems day in and day out.

Trading psychologist Bennett McDowell suggests in an online article that a humble, submissive posture toward the power of the markets is of much greater benefit than an aggressive stance. He writes:

> Some new traders who had to be aggressive in their chosen businesses tend to think they need to be aggressive with the markets. It seems logical. In fact, that is what made them successful before as sales people, managers, executives, doctors, business owners, entrepreneurs, etc. In trading however, this aggressive type of behavior can actually be your biggest weakness. The belief that you can force the market to do what you want and make your trade work, just won't happen! The markets are too big. In fact some of the most successful traders I know approach the market passively! They tend to "Follow" the markets and not force an outcome.

Again, learn this maxim: "*Let the markets do what they want to do!*" This book gives you the tools necessary to do just that *and* earn a great living from them. In truth, trend trading is really all about *trend following*. You will note that in nearly every setup we offer here, a trend is already in place—either in price, in the indicators, or in both—before we enter the trade. The prideful trader wants to glory in trying to outthink the markets, to buy when everyone is selling and to sell when everyone is buying in the hopes of catching the reversal before anyone else sees it. But unless you have insider information, or you are as business savvy as a Warren Buffett or a Peter Lynch, it is best to stick with what works. What works in trend trading is a humble posture toward the market, letting it tell us as clearly as possible what it is likely to do next.

Another area where pride needs to be swallowed and humility adopted is that of sticking firmly to your trading systems. Let me give you an example from one of the worst trades I've made in recent memory. While my trading systems normally require that we sell prior to an earnings announcement, I decided to hold one of my positions over the announcement in the hope that the company, like it did in the previous two quarters, would beat Street estimates. The company closed trading at a price of 25.48, a full +12 percent over our entry price. Our subscribers happily logged their nice gain and moved on. I, however, woke the next morning to find the same stock trading below 20.00 after both earnings per share (EPS) and guidance came in below the Street. And when the dip buyers failed to come to my rescue (the stock traded briefly under 18.00), I finally sold my position for a very embarrassing loss.

This kind of agonizing mistake happens even to the best of traders, but it cannot happen to successful traders very often. What caused me to hold overnight? Well, greed, pure and simple, yes, but also pride—the prideful attitude that led me to believe that I knew better than my own trading systems. Imagine that! So in short, for the sake of your trading success, adopt a humble attitude toward both the markets and your various trading disciplines. Both know better than you do.

DR. STOXX'S BIG VISION: MAKE EVERYONE A TRADER

Several years ago I sat in a commuter's café in New York City's Grand Central Station with my brother-in-law, Tony. As the caffeine began to whirl in our brains, we talked of our mutual love for trading and how we both were looking for ways to take our trading to the next level. By that time I had developed most of the systems taught in this book, and my online trading store, Befriendthetrend.com, had just been launched. Tony is a computer programmer, among other things (including owning his own ISP), and he suggested that there might be a way to automate my nightly research routine. He described the possibility of software that would screen for each of our setups, suggest entry prices and stop-losses, and even connect to an OLB to send in the trade orders automatically. In this way, you could truly trade for a living while being completely occupied with some other activity (such as your day job).

That conversation never did get much further than that, unfortunately. I am still waiting for Tony to sell his business and devote himself full-time to programming our software. But the conversation started me thinking of ways I could expand the outreach of our services. Over the next year, I began writing up various how-to manuals on different trading strategies including swing trading, day trading, and e-minis trading. All of these have sold very well over the years, and they are still hard to keep in stock. Then we held a four-hour online seminar for over 200 beginning traders. The seminar was so successful, we put on a second seminar for intermediate to advanced traders the next month. Soon I started getting calls from traders to serve as their personal trading coach. Then came requests that I set up a hedge fund for our clients who were too busy to trade for themselves. So we did, and the Befriend the Trend Fund was born (now approaching its fourth year). Then there were requests for articles to trading publications. And now this book. In short, my passion for trading quite quickly became a small cottage industry.

Now, as we head into our seventh year in business at Befriendthetrend.com, I find myself asking, "What's next? Where does the dream go from here?" Well, I'm not sure where it *will* go from here, but I can tell you where I'd *like* it to go. Let me in summary form lay out a vision of where I hope to see the trend-trading phenomenon go over the next decade (and Befriendthetrend.com along with it).

Trading Centers

I'd love to see the development of trading and educational centers across the United States and abroad. I'm not talking here about the notorious "prop shops" of the 1990s, so many of which either went bankrupt or were indicted for fraud. What I envision instead is a series of franchise-worthy storefronts, located in suburban shopping malls as well as downtown business districts, that would house trading stations, plenty of flat panels showing financial news, and overhead monitors to flash market updates and charts of interest on large screens. These would be cool, hip places—

with attention paid to interior design—where traders could hang out together, talk stocks, trade their accounts, and along the way, learn a thing or two. Managers of each center would be highly adept at technical analysis and reading between the lines of money flow and would be available to traders for advice and training. Stocks showing promising technical setups would be called out over loudspeakers and their charts flashed up on the screens. In back rooms, seminars would be taught each day for those wanting to strengthen their trading skills. Espresso would be served during market hours and then microbrews after the close. Heck, forget about trading; it would just be a lot of fun to hang out there, wouldn't it?

I'm not sure what the best business plan would be to make sure these centers are profitable. Perhaps they could come under the wing of some of the bigger Wall Street banks as an extension of their private client services. What's in it for them? A number of things: increased customer base, enhanced customer loyalty, positive branding (think Goldman Sachs meets Starbucks), investment diversification (through owning commercial property), and certainly an increase in commission revenue, to name a few. Monthly membership fees, a cut on the commission structure, and sales from beverages, music, seminars, and educational materials would likely make the individual shops an attractive franchise.

Automated Money Machines

Well, one problem with the trading centers idea is that market hours are usually when everyone has to work, doggone it. Not everyone can (yet) trade for a living. Some of us have to keep the old day job. So who is going to spend time there on a Tuesday morning at 10 a.m.? Mostly retirees and the unemployed, both groups that tend not to have the kind of discretionary funds needed to open a trading account.

So here is an alternative that would also serve the same purpose of bringing more people into the trading game: build software for use at home that would completely automate the trading process. If we can find a way to mechanize the setup screening, and if we can find a way to enter orders automatically, and if the same software can then update those orders at each market close, in effect we will have created an automatic money machine. We will have turned all my years of hard work into a regular ATM.

Is this possible? Sure it is. Currently there exist chart pattern recognition software, technical parameter screening software, and automated order entry and order management systems. Why couldn't all these be put together into a single package? Why couldn't we design software to (1) determine the general market type (as mentioned previously), (2) screen for trade setups to match the market type, and (3) enter and exit those setups automatically, in hands-off fashion? Certainly this can be done. Any software engineers out there in need of a job?

Okay, there is one glaring problem facing the creation and marketing of such a trading machine. Let's say we were successful in building an automatic money machine that would screen for and trade only the most fitting of all our trend-trading setups. And let's say we then wanted to offer this software to the public. So we hire a top-notch advertising firm and get the word out. We put on e-mail campaigns; we send out direct-mail fliers; we buy radio and even television time. And soon the orders come streaming in. We sell 500 copies . . . and then 1,000 . . . and then word of mouth kicks in and we are quickly up to 5,000, then 10,000. Then we make a few refinements, bring out the 2.0 version, and sell another 10,000 copies. So now there are 20,000 traders out there using our money machine to trade their accounts automatically. That's a reasonable figure for a piece of software that might retail for around $2,000 (plus the monthly data fee).

Do you see where this is going? Let me spell it out. Say the machine issues a signal to buy KLAC at 50.00 per share. KLAC is a pretty heavily traded stock. The average number of shares traded is around 5 million per day. But look what happens when 20,000 traders get the same signal to buy KLAC at 50.00 per share. If each trader takes an average position of 500 shares (some a lot more, some a lot less), that makes for 10 million shares aiming at a single entry price of 50.00. That's over twice the average daily volume trying to enter the market in the *first minute* of trading. Is that going to happen? No way. Either KLAC will gap up and over 50.00 and not look back, or it will gap open at 50.00, run up a bit, then collapse once all that volume is assimilated. Neither scenario provides a profitable trading environment.

Is there a solution? Yes there is, and it's called diversification. We need to come up with not one money machine but *dozens* of them. We need to have money machines for day traders, scalpers, swing traders, overnight and position traders; for those with high-risk and those with low-risk tolerances; for large account and small account traders; for professional money managers; and for the average Joe trading his IRA. Then come the sector money machines, the ETF money machines, the e-mini money machines, the Forex money machines—and on and on it goes. In this way we spread the wealth, the order flow, and, hence, the risk as well.

Personal Trading Coaches Network

One last dream I have for trend trading over the next decade is to establish a network of personal trading coaches. These coaches would be trained at one of several training facilities (see the trading centers idea mentioned previously) to serve individual traders in need of private coaching. And why not? Today we have fitness coaches, weight loss coaches, childbirth coaches, and motivation coaches. We hire coaches to help us learn how to cook, knit, do yoga, and get closer to God. Why not hire a coach to help us learn how to trade?

I envision a network of dedicated, licensed professional traders who, as a means to supplement their income, would travel to the client's home for a series of one-on-one sessions. In this private setting, every aspect of trading could be covered, from setting up the watch lists to screening out the best trades. Higher-level skills such as tape reading, spread trading, and hedging could be taught to more advanced clients. And all clients would benefit from various trading visualization exercises led by the coach in order to bolster the healthy trader's mindset.

I know that this kind of one-on-one mentoring really works well for taking a mediocre trader, even a losing trader, to a high level of trading success. I've been privileged to coach several of our clients personally, in their homes at their own computers, and have found it to be a very rewarding teaching experience. Certainly it is the most efficient way to convey trading knowledge. Often it is simply a matter of spotting one thing the trader was doing wrong and then suggesting a remedy. In other cases it is a matter of doing some serious structural work on the entire trading system. However the coaching proceeds, it is a wonderfully effective process, and I would like to see it become more and more accessible.

FINAL THOUGHTS

T REND-TRADING stocks and options can be one of the most exciting, and certainly one of the most challenging, hobbies you can have. Over time, and with the right education and experience, it can become a very profitable hobby—so profitable, in fact, that you can make a very nice living from it and never have to hold a real job again (unless you consider sitting in front of a computer and clicking a mouse now and then a real job). I believe that you now hold in your hands all you need to know to take your trading to the highest levels of success. Trend trading is right at the sweet spot of what trading is all about, and this book is your key to learning how to trend-trade.

Trend trading can be the means to many wonderful and important ends, but as soon as it becomes your *raison d'etre*, you have lost the battle for balance. Here is a test: What is the first thing you think about when you wake up? What is the last thing you think about as you drift off to sleep at night? Is it the same thing? And is that thing trading? Now here is a warning: if your first and last thoughts of the day are about trading, then trading for you is no longer a hobby—*it is an addiction*.

It is natural (and I'm speaking from experience) to be so excited about your trading successes that the joy and hope of it all color everything else you do with a resplendent glory. It is likewise natural (again from experience) to feel so despondent about your trading failures that everything else you do is burdened by a dark melancholy. If you do not have some means of getting beyond this emotional roller coaster, of living a life of stable productivity despite what the market does, it is perhaps best if you do not take up trading at all. Or better yet: determine right now to build into yourself the kind of character that can function well, relate well, and in every way *be* well regardless of what the market does with your money.

You now know where to open your online trading account, which charting package to use, how to set up your charts and watch lists, how to scan and screen each day for viable setups, how to whittle your results down to the best one or two setups each day, and at what price to enter and exit your trades. You also have a variety of resources that should help you develop the sort of mental approach to your trading that will allow you to follow our guidelines. This is a complete system. Study the setups in this book until their various parameters are memorized. Then apply them rigorously, and watch as slowly, over time, your account begins to blossom.

I want to leave you with three final thoughts.

The first is this: be patient with yourself and with your trading. Trend trading is not by any means a get-rich-quick scheme, but it potentially is a get-rich-slow scheme. You will see net gains over time. Over the long haul (and I mean years, not months), you will see substantial gains. Stick with this system for a lifetime and you may very well see phenomenal gains.

The second is this: there is always room in every trader's toolbox for ingenuity. While I've made every effort to make our 10 trading setups and our options systems as mechanical as possible, 1,000 traders reading this book and applying our 10 setups will not come up with the same stocks to trade. There is room for interpretation, even experimentation within the basic parameters. It is important to find what you are most comfortable with, what best suits your temperament and lifestyle, and then stick with that. And that sticking-to-it-ness really is the key: once you have your system established, stick with it!

The third is this: you can do it! No matter what language you speak, where you went to school, how much money you have to start with (okay, that one matters a little), you can open a trading account, buy a few shares, put on stop-loss and target orders, and make some money. Don't let fear get in your way.

If confusion is now your obstacle, then that is my fault and I am wholeheartedly sorry. Write me, "Dr Stoxx," at support@befriendthetrend.com if you have any questions. I am always here to help. God bless you in all your endeavors, and especially as you *trend-trade for a living!*

INDEX

ABOUT THE AUTHOR

Dr. Thomas Carr, or Dr. Stoxx, as he is widely known in the trading community, has been actively involved in the markets since 1996, following several years of studying technical analysis. He holds a master's of divinity degree from Princeton Theological Seminary, and master's and doctorate degrees in philosophy and theology from Oxford University. In addition to trading and managing a small hedge fund, Dr. Carr is a tenured professor of religious studies and philosophy at Mount Union College in Ohio. He has been interviewed by the *Wall Street Journal* and *U.S. News and World Report* for his insights into trading psychology. His previous publications on trading have appeared in *Active Trader* and *Technical Analysis of Stocks and Commodities*. Dr. Carr is also the author of the popular textbook, *Introducing Death and Dying* (2005: Prentice-Hall).

Dr. Stoxx began trading as a part-time hobby until two years of losses forced him to do more research. He attended several trading seminars and studied under some of the top names in the business, including Alexander Elder, Steve Nison, and Welles Wilder. Soon he began experimenting with his own trading systems. The result was a set of time-tested, proprietary trading methods that have proved to be very profitable in all types of market conditions. These systems are based on the essentials of technical analysis but also incorporate Dr. Stoxx's unique method of assessing market psychology, sector strength, and general market directionality. Highly skilled as a tape reader, Dr. Stoxx possesses an uncanny ability to time his entries and exits, often just prior to major moves. Dr. Stoxx is CEO of Befriend the Trend Trading, a Web-based advisory and trading education service (www.befriendthetrend.com). He also serves as general partner of a capital management company that provides wealth-creating opportunities for accredited investors.

Dr. Stoxx lives with his wife and two daughters in northeastern Ohio. He is in frequent demand as a seminar speaker and private trading coach. For booking information, please send enquiries to drstoxx@befriendthetrend.com.